Adoption Reunion
in the Social Media Age,
An Anthology

Edited by Laura Dennis

Entourage Publishing
2014

Entourage Publishing
Redondo Beach, CA 90278

We would love your feedback! Send comments to
laura@adoptedrealitymemoir.com
www.laura-dennis.com

Adoption Reunion in the Social Media Age,
An Anthology, edited and compiled by Laura Dennis

Entourage Publishing e-books
1st edition 2014 eISBN: 978-0-9856168-4-7
Paperback ISBN: 978-0-9856168-5-4

Cover Art by Linda Boulanger (2014)
Tell-Tale Book Cover Designs

Praise for
Adoption Reunion in the Social Media Age, An Anthology

Have you ever clicked on a link and received the error message, "HTTP Code: 404 Not Found"? You experience a jolt, a moment of disbelief, and irritation. Perhaps you are disappointed that you can't get the information you need. When this happens to me, I will often click on the link several times to convince myself that it really doesn't work.

Welcome to the life of the adoptee.

The broken hyperlink is, I believe, an appropriate metaphor for an adoptee's life. By virtue of nearly universal laws and practices based on shame, denial and misinformation, most adoptees have a broken link at their earliest beginnings. A broken link to their blood, to their heritage, to their ancestry, to their medical history and to the core of their very identity.

The stories in this anthology are written by brave souls who have dug deep into the source code hidden behind their broken links. Who have looked behind the unreal facade of the "happily ever after" adoption fairy tale, and repaired the links to their identity. Their stories inform, illuminate and provide hope to the millions of adoptees (and I might venture, their biological/first parents) who wish to do the same.

It is no accident that the interconnectedness created

by the Internet is facilitating the repair of broken connections in the lives of adoptees. This e-book itself is a shining example of repair-in-action. The authors have become connected through the Internet and their truth telling is being further disseminated and shared through this medium.

Anyone seeking to repair their own broken links, to find the source code to their own lives, will be inspired, educated and moved to tears, smiles and laughter by these heartfelt and heart-rending stories. We are born to be connected. HTTP Code 200: Page Found.

— Karen Caffrey, LPC, JD

*　*　*

The anthology, *Adoption Reunion in the Social Media Age*, reveals the emotionally complex challenges inherent in adoption. The reader will find pieces of themselves in every story. Probing questions after each story serve to help the reader delve deeper and gain greater awareness of their own personal narrative. Especially recommended for anyone considering or in the midst of search and reunion.

— Carol Schaefer, Author of *The Other Mother*

*　*　*

I can remember as I started my searches for birth family members that any time I came across someone else story, I had to read it. I was always looking for could mine turn out like that? What did they do to find someone? What were the mistakes and pitfalls that others took so I can try to avoid them! Of course, as most of us who search know, your own story always has its own unique quirks and twists. Yet, it's still so helpful to read about how others have navigated this strange and murky world of finding those who share your genetics and carry your story.

Anyone who faces a reunion struggles to find a guide, or step by step, or instruction manual for how to do it and how to do it well. Those who have experienced reunion know all too well that there is never one set of instructions or guidelines that will fit for everyone. The opportunity to read a wide range of different experiences and stories is useful and interesting. This book allows the reader to quickly see a range of experiences, different thoughts, ideas and feelings and different outcomes for adoption reunions. Since no one can predict how anyone's search will end, Ms. Dennis' book is a great place to start imagining the variety of outcomes you could experience. I enjoyed the variety of experiences described and the wide range of stories and reactions.

— Rebecca Ricardo, LCSW, Executive Director coordinators2inc The Lifetime Adoption Resource, adoptee and birth mother

✳ ✳ ✳

An excellent resource for anyone separated by adoption—adoptee or birth parent— whether they are considering reunion or not, or are faced with being found. Contributors are all excellent writers and share their experiences in ways that are very relatable.

—Mirah Riben, Author of *The Stork Market: America's Multi-Billion Dollar Unregulated Adoption Industry*

For the voiceless,

the silenced,

and the secret-holders' victims,

We stand with you.

Contents

Introduction:

Connected

By Laura Dennis

Perhaps it is slightly unorthodox to have the introduction written by the editor. But hey, unorthodox is what I do. I also "do" critical thinking, often in a blunt (some would say sarcastic) manner. Accordingly, I fit in swimmingly among my fellow adoptees (Who would have thought?). If there is one thing that I've learned about the adoption community, it is that B.S. tolerance is extremely low, propensity for questioning, wondering and dreaming; high. All of that's a good thing. It's through this adoption community that I was inspired to seek out the essays you'll read in *Adoption Reunion in the Social Media Age, An Anthology*.

But first, let me qualify: the adoption community to which I refer is not necessarily the one mainstream society is accustomed to. I'm not a part of the "Are you experiencing an unplanned pregnancy? Have you considered adoption?" community. Nor am I a part of the "Birth mothers who give away their babies are selfless for wanting their child to have a better life with a deserving adoptive couple," community. Not even the "I'm so grateful to my adoptive parents for adopting me, and never need to search" community.

The adoption community I'm a part of recognizes the pain in adoption. It sees the need for change in adoption as an institution. It understands the deep desire adoptees have to know our roots, to search and reunite whenever possible. The adoption community I'm a part of actively and passionately debates the nuances, the triumphs and the frustrations. My entry into this community came by way of Amanda H.L. Transue-Woolston, who blogs at The Declassified Adoptee, and who founded the blogging community, The Lost Daughters. Hence, it was only all the more appropriate that she write the Afterword for this anthology—her essay brings together all of the contributors' experiences with an inspiring call-to-action. You see, I couldn't be more grateful to her for inviting me into the Lost Daughters tribe; a place where for the first time, my "adoptee-ness"—and all its attendant triggers, questions and issues—is completely within the range of normal. What a relief!

From my connection to The Lost Daughters, many

of whom are contributors here, I expanded my awareness to the blogs, books and writings of first mothers, adoptive parents and mental health professionals who are dedicated to expanding awareness of ways to improve adoption as an institution. I had my mind blown by the writings of Daniel Drennan, who wrote the thought-provoking Foreword for this anthology.

However, I must point out that, for me, an American mother with young (non-adopted) children who lives in Serbia of all places; this community exists almost completely online. In other words, I came to all of this education by way of social media, blogs, and online communities.

This connection, I believe, is the wave of the future.

When I was growing up in a closed adoption, the only person who I knew who was adopted was my adoptive brother, someone who would prefer not to search. I knew no one, absolutely no one like me; who wanted, who *needed* to search for her first family. Who felt a connection to her first mom, even though she had no conscious knowledge of such a woman. Even when I searched, I still knew NO other adoptees who were searching, let alone reuniting.

But that's changing, and this anthology is meant to be a resource for the next wave of adoptees—in closed and open adoptions, who will navigate reunion over the long haul. (And yeah, it is a long haul, a lot of work, and not all flowers and sunshine.)

You may be wondering, How do I know who these people are, that they're not just making this stuff up?

I would turn the question around ... How well do we really know people IRL (in real life)? How much do others hide their true selves, keep secrets—even if they are "just" sins by omission?

It's true that many people hide behind their online personas and use their computers as a means to create an alternate self, a reality that is better, richer, and more successful than the one they live. But in this case, it's my view that social media has allowed members to come more fully into being. By connecting with like-minded individuals across continents and oceans, we have found kindred souls. We have found people who challenge us, who empathize with us, and who want to learn from us.

Just because I've not had the pleasure or opportunity to meet these writers in person, doesn't mean that they have not been carefully vetted. Several of these contributors have books, most have blogs. I have read all of it. I've connected with these writers, with people who know them, and many have become close personal friends. And one day, when I don't live in Serbia, I hope and wish and dream to meet them in person.

But now, with access to information, to social media ... no longer will we be in the dark, wondering if there are others "out there" like us. There *is* a community of like-minded individuals, emerging from their own personal adoption fog, trying to make sense of this adoptee life.

These are people, yes real people!, who have personally helped me through complicated family situations, tough decisions, and of course, those tricky-yet-sometimes-devastating emotional triggers. It was these types of online discussions that inspired the Clarity Questions at the end of each essay. It was the gentle and understanding prompting of those who had been—or were currently—in my very shoes, guiding my understanding of myself and how adoption affects my life. These Clarity Questions are designed to inspire the reader to think how the contributor's article could relate to their own personal experience, or to an adoptee they know. They are written primarily by me—with contributor input, and are meant to be the antithesis of the adoption fog. (If you're not familiar with this phrase, keep reading; it's a running theme in this book.)

The reality is that in this adoption community of which I'm so privileged to be a part, we exist to support one others' searches, cry when we experience rejection, and laugh when it all seems like too much. Those who have never seen this community firsthand often have a hard time understanding that all of these relationships occur online. Again, I say: Wave of the future. This is the reality of life today; and it is amazing. Adoption reunion can and does occur in the social media age (how can it not?), and this anthology is not only an amalgamation of experiences that have happened in the new millennium with the help of the Internet, it is a *direct result* of my own personal online interaction with the adoption community. I'm so thankful for each and every contributor and their time, effort and energy in helping this anthology come to fruition. So, really, how could the anthology *not* be called, *Adoption Reunion in the Social Media Age*?

The purpose of this book is to give voice to the wide experiences of adoptees and those who love them, examining the emotional, psychological and logistical effects of adoption reunion. Primarily adult adoptee voices, we also hear from adoptive parents, first moms and mental health professionals, all weighing in on their experience with reunion. The stories run the gamut, and I think even non-adopted people are likely to find something in here to which they can relate. The memories of adoption reunion in this anthology are joyous and regretful; nostalgic and fresh; angry and accepting. They show pain, but they also tell of resilience and strength in the face of incredible loss.

In short, the essays of this anthology relate the human experience: raw, resilient, and most of all real.

Laura Dennis was born and adopted in New Jersey and raised in Maryland. She earned a B.A. and M.F.A. in dance performance and choreography, but gave up aches and pains and bloody feet in 2004 to become a stylish, sales director for a biotech startup. Then with two children under the age of three, in 2010 she and her husband sought to simplify their lifestyle and escaped to his hometown, Belgrade. While the children learned Serbian in their cozy preschool, Laura recovered from sleep deprivation and wrote *Adopted Reality, A Memoir*, available on Amazon. She blogs at www.laura-dennis.com.

Foreword:

The Seeker and the Sought

By Daniel Drennan

In those early days of my return to the place of my origin, I spent much time at my former orphanage: searching, seeking, hunting; for references, for clues, for my story. I believed my efforts would help me to understand and come to terms with my adoption a half century earlier; that there were straightforward answers to my myriad questions; that perseverance would be rewarded. Barring any ability to know the definite place of my birth, the orphanage became a de facto starting point; a return to source. My research into the documents and file folders I came across there was a way to overlook the fact that my own dossier inexplicably went missing. Even worse, the paperwork I did hold—full of falsified names and untruths—brought me no closer to a resolution of my yearning for reunion. And so my journey started, on quite shaky ground.

I diverted myself while there by photographing the interior of the once bustling care center, now empty. Similarly I documented the city I now called home; as well as the country I ironically found myself a stranger returned to. If photographs serve as replacement memories, then perhaps it were possible to recapture my might-have-been past by grabbing onto and preserving the present. I gave myself over to my new acculturation, excruciatingly forcing myself into situations of incomprehension and misunderstanding, attempting to apprehend the complexities of a language that should have been mine by birth. Out of sheer necessity, I became an astute observer, absorbing every nuance of culture, language, and social exchange, in an immersion that was painful for both its odd and fleeting resonance, as well as a creeping sense of the inability to truly return.

Every once in a while I would venture back to this ersatz starting point in the company of a fellow adoptee, who acted as a foil between me and the few nuns who remained on staff there. They would speak to her about me in the third person, quizzing her as to my motives; I dutifully ignored them. Instead, given the absence of concrete facts concerning my case, I focused all of my attention onto the narratives of others, bureaucratically stowed away between their manila covers, and hidden inside dusty steel file cabinets. I would compare them to my own tremulous narrative: Against all odds I had managed to weave one out of the wan threads gleaned from the nuns, from my adoptive parents' recollections, as well as via the meanderings of my own imagination.

My story as I understood it growing up finds my parents in the Beirut airport during the last leg of their tour of the Holy Land, meeting up with some orphanage staff who were seeing off a baby adopted to France, and to whom they explained their desire to adopt. They were told to return the next week and there would be a child waiting for them. In stark contrast, the official narrative was one of abject abandonment. I was reportedly left on the beach of Dbayeh north of Beirut, Lebanon, found by a policeman, and brought to the convent in Dakwaneh, and from there to the orphanage in Achrafieh. I'm inclined not to believe this version, for various cultural as well as circumstantial reasons. More likely mine is a story of coercion, procurement, trafficking, and brokering; but this has always been a taboo subject, and so remains not just unspoken, but a non-thought; pointless to even bring up.

Somewhere in the mirror reflection of these second-hand stories lie the narratives of those whose experience is relegated to nothing much more than an indirect triviality. I have spent the last ten years trying to account for this as best as I can, and this despite the evident impossibility of such action. On top of the psychological pain this has caused, it seems I am fated to likewise suffer for the distress my search brings to those who see it as a rebuke or worse, even though I have never framed it this way. It leaves me on the defensive concerning something I never stated or expressed in any way; it weighs me down with much in the way of added baggage. The path of my journey thus became a rocky one; travelled more-or-less alone; without much to guide me; sapping of energy.

"Why does Daniel want to search? What is he looking for? Why isn't he happy with what he has? What is he hoping to find? There is nothing to be found by looking!"

So the sisters would express their despair to my friend as I tried my best to maneuver my way without their help, growing more upset myself, saddened and angry, forced yet again to listen to such words which, in various permutations and from a variety of sources, had filled my head my entire life. For my own sanity, I decided that the goal of the search was not important, but the searching itself; a Zen-like compromise in which the destination was sidelined for the sake and safety of the sojourner. In this way reunion was put off into a distant utopian future that might—or more likely, might not—transpire.

This "plateau" seems to have served me well, despite the fact that I am so near (physically speaking) and yet so far away from anything resembling an answer. I distanced myself (and was likewise distanced from) the class of those I initially thought would be most supportive of me. At the same time, I have managed to bond further with many locally speaking with whom I share little in terms of my adoptive acculturation. They have become a support system of no small import. I cut off contact with the orphanage; it took too much of a psychological toll, especially as I learned more about the functional aspect of what we refer to generically as "orphanages" and their economic and political role in society. I was discovering information--concerning trafficking, brokering, warehousing, mistreatment, as well as euthanizing of children--that I would not wish knowing on my worst enemy. At the same time, there did exist here orphanages that managed to communally and properly care for children, giving the lie to the myth of nuclear family and its universality, as well as to adoption itself.

For relief and solace I turned again to similar narratives in various stages of unfolding, seeking evidences and commonalities. As I experienced the blogs, books, articles, and documentaries of those whose lives have been affected by various displacements including adoption, I was comforted with the understanding that others have previously explored this territory. I have not limited myself to stories of just other adoptees, but to anyone who has undergone an adoption-related life-change, and beyond that, to those equally displaced and dispossessed against their will. The spectrum of such voices is vast, and the stories related range from outright acceptance to utter rejection of our various lots in life, and I appreciate this immensely; for I've traveled this journey of extremes myself.

I do not mean to express by this the oft-voiced trope that "everyone is entitled to their own opinion." We are not talking mere points of view, although there are political, ethical, and moral debates to be had concerning the subject at hand. To reduce life-stories to just so much "opinionated back and forth" is an injustice in and of itself, as well as a narrative cop-out which shuts off listening to the voices of others, though it feigns otherwise. I refute this categorically. No, I wish to emphasize that it is invalid to see these as individual recountings battling for dominance along static and divisive lines. Instead, they form a dynamic, expansive, and much greater narrative, not just of our lives which remain interconnected via adoption, but also beyond this to others who have lived similar experiences.

Locally here in Lebanon, this has been brought home to me by those whose lives are now intertwined with mine along these very similar lines: refugees, migrant workers, marginalized populations, to name a few. I have settled in with these groups because of our shared circumstances which are based in common notions of separation, distance from family, and removal from originating place. I have taken great comfort from those who inherently understand my story when I relate it to them. Their response, which usually focuses on the injustice of being so displaced, is a welcome relief from the usual "you were lucky" or "you were chosen" that dogged me growing up, and which was echoed by the community of my orphanage. Beyond all of this, I never thought I might be so welcomed back; no one was more surprised by this reception than I. For this welcome I am eternally grateful, and I can only hope to one day be able to repay my debt of gratitude.

Yet such a welcome should not have surprised me; the blind spot here is wholly mine. For in fact, it makes perfect sense if we examine the purely functional aspect of adoption economically and politically speaking: a leveraging of social inequality (however it might manifest itself) in a procurement of children from those who have, to provide them to those who have not. Here I am speaking purely in terms of situational fact, without any judgment implied. In defining adoption in this way, we are made aware of others who have equally been displaced and dispossessed against their will. I state this in the hope of finding a common starting point that speaks of adoption beyond the purely personal and individual level. To do so requires a moving beyond inherently unequal concepts (deceptively defined otherwise) of triad, constellation, mosaic, etc. We might refer to this as the search for an even playing field; an open and level plain to meet and converge upon.

Underlying this are basic notions of power differential as well as of agency, which flow along a similar continuum of individual to communal. By this I mean to say that our sense of free will is defined and shaped by a variety of outside incentives, pressures, encouragements, dissuasions, and other derivations— familial, communal, societal, spiritual, etc.—which we can say helped us form a decision, or which we might say held sway outside of our control, or which played a role somewhere in between, or, yet again, which we might be completely ignorant of. Similar to countries going through a reconciliation process, it is not valid to maintain such power differentials, or unequal agency. And so, for example, it is not enough to hear an apology from those who nonetheless remain in control: There is an inherent need for all stories to be heard in a way that truly empowers the tellers as a whole, that incorporates them into the body politic. That some stories from the realm of adoption are encouraged while others are met with disdain reveals the power differential and disempowerment so involved.

At the same time, I do not wish to form false separations based on such power differentials; I am instead stating that there need be a balanced retelling, and one that is empowering to those on the downhill or external side as it were. Meaning, outside of the framework of those who dominate the given domains of narrative power: the academy, the media and publishing worlds, the legal realm, just to name a few. There is much in the way of equalizing that need take place; a bridging of common ground. For example, it is a small step to apply a similar definition of separation from place implied by "adoption" to many of the families we are thus connected to: often from immigrant stock, and beyond this, often further displaced due to suburbanization, or work requirements, or any of the other economic and political reasons that see people moving away from home and originating place; estranged from what was formerly known. Here we push into "unspoken of" narrative causations; the shadowy recesses of our interwoven stories desperate for illumination.

It is at this point I would like to shift slightly our notion of "reunion" and what it means. We often think of reunion as being a reconnecting with other *people*, and we are forced to judge the success or failure of such reunion on the basis of the personal relationships so re-established. When viewed in this binary "either-or" way, we are bound to suffer the accusations that we are "ungrateful," "bitter," "jaded," and "angry," as if searching for one family or community detracts or takes away from another; a zero-sum game of affinity and affiliation. Viewed this way, such reunions are destined to fail, especially if both sides are equally "lost," or likewise on unstable ground, and this for similar cultural, societal, economic, and political reasons that go unmentioned. And so, some food for thought: What if reunion is as much of place as it is of people? And what if reunion on the personal level need be prefaced by a literal "grounding" of those coming together in this way? An arrival on equal footing, a restful landing for all those involved? A leveling of site as well as relational hierarchy?

I ask this because many of our narratives focus on this idea of searching for "something"; a feeling of endlessly "looking" in the hopes of "finding"... here we trail off to an abyss-like ellipsis. To understand is that "to search" implies a quest that is definable, nameable, even if unknowable, or intangible: "The search for the Holy Grail," for example. Yet often our searches seem to explicitly stress on the undefinable—"searching for something"—which is a phrase most often used by the forgetful. "I got up and went into the bedroom, but I forgot what I was looking for; but I knew I was searching for *something*." Even here, benefit of the doubt is given to the one searching; their relation to place or space is not questioned, and the object of the search, though forgotten, still exists in its unnamed state.

It is, on the other hand, not possible to define the feeling of "searching" when you have no connection to what it is you are searching for, much less a relationship to the places you might search. By this I mean to say that the "groundedness" of being of a place allows us both to explore that place, as well as "go off searching" elsewhere, sure of our return. We can apply similar logic to trips and destinations: I might very well say, "I'm going to the store" or "to the movies," implying that I am sure of where I am, of where I'm going, and of how I'll get there and back. But it is much rarer (and infinitely more sad on some level) to say: "I'm getting in the car and am going to drive, but I don't know where to"; or "I'm leaving, but I don't know where I'm going or how I'll get there"; or "This place is hostile, or toxic, or unwelcoming; I can no longer remain here."

Without that connection, searching takes on an existential significance, and it is this lack of grounding that leaves us in a paradoxical state; a middling nowhere; a never-ending quest; in Limbo. We are treading quicksand at this point. This is compounded if we equalize our perspective and see those around us— seemingly comfortable in their place—as being just as much on shaky ground as we are. Does our distancing ourselves from this—the first footfall away from which sets us off "searching" whether we admit it or not—does this not form the basis of what we refer to as "giving up the Kool-Aid," of "coming out of the fog"? Personally speaking, I feel somehow that this (subconsciously understood) difference explains my hesitance in searching further for family in Lebanon: I first needed to establish footing; grounding. To stand strong—literally steadfast— requires first that this "stead"—this sense of place and the place itself—be secured.

The nuns at my orphanage would often castigate me with the phrase: "There's no happy ending to be found here, Daniel; no reunion has been a good one; be happy with what you have; stop searching." I fear they tragically miss the point, and their reaction is puzzling, if not infuriating. Have they not similarly been distanced from their far-afield towns in Syria to work and serve in Beirut their entire lives? Have they not likewise been acculturated out of an originating language, now speaking the French of the colonizer of these countries? In another vein, can they continue to ignore the populations of Lebanon whose status as Peoples is premised on originating place, and the promise of Return thereto? From this vantage point, can I not say the same thing of my adoptive father, third-generation Irish-American, equally estranged from place and culture and language? How did we manage to not find a bond here? Is this, perhaps, the basis of the resistance to our searching, a realization of what they, too, have lost, or have given up, now reflected in our need to seek that which remains for them unseekable? The unintended consequence of their resistance is that their denial of our search's validity only emphasizes all the more the exact opposite: to search is to be on a valid path. One may choose to not go down this path, but its inherent validity cannot be denied.

I am often asked: "What is the point of speaking out in this way? To what purpose?" This is a cynical and baneful question, and I used to despair of an answer. But now the response is clear to me. There is no individual goal in my searching, but a communal one; my quest is not uniquely personal, and will not end should I, God willing, be successful. For I wonder: what if the file cabinet at my orphanage could speak? If all the files inside spoke aloud? Its walls, its stones, its doors, the ghosts of those who walked its halls allowed witness? What if our voices were to echo and resonate with others seeking "place," searching for "reunion," however defined; a multitude of stories, destined to change and morph and expand with time and reflection, but nonetheless needing to be told in their entirety? A tidal wave of testifying? To this point, in reading the narratives that follow in this anthology, I would only ask that we reflect on them not as static documents now relegated to history and the past, but as living testimony, continuous, forming branches and webs of connections to other stories, and all of them ending not in finalizing punctuation but instead in ellipses of our own design, as much as they often began in a similarly unknowable way, quite beyond our control.

Looking back, I recollect that at a certain point of my life here in Beirut it evidenced itself to me, this shift from being vaguely "in" a place to being more solidly "of" it. Without thinking about it, I had stopped blogging and explaining this life to those outside of it. More importantly, I had stopped photographing, was no longer documenting, attempting to capture, to fix. I was no longer an outsider, and needed to drop the affectations of one from the outside. My life expanded backward once again in time, even back to that earliest month that remains unknown and perhaps unknowable. My acculturation came forward and I acknowledged it for the affectation I now see it as, just as much as I had attempted to overcome it or forego it; to forget it. I endeavored to understand that my narrative as such was shared by a majority of the planet, in various forms and permutations, and this collective whole was infinitely more valid and validating of my sense of self than my personal forays into dark tunnels and down dead-end streets.

I liken this situation to an absent individual puzzle piece, whose shape is formed by focusing instead on that which surrounds it, no less visible despite what goes missing. Such a shift in focus eases the sense of what often seems to be a "lonely journey," and forms the basis for much in the way of common cause. Having been reunited with place, I feel I can now deal with attempting a reunion of the popular and familial kind. In an effort to reconcile things, I revisited the orphanage last year, and this time the nuns ecstatically addressed me in our original language, Arabic, and I was informed that I understand now where they are coming from, culturally speaking. This is true, I do; all the same, I do not absolve them, or, for that matter, anyone who played a role in our situations, of their duty and obligation to understand our need for seeking, for searching, despite not always knowing what it is we are looking for. This is their burden to assume; their part of the bargain.

Perhaps it was too much to expect the nuns, themselves distanced from our stories via a generation passed, and likewise tied up in their own imbalanced hierarchies and mythologies, their own affectations of power and status, to "understand" our searching. In this light, they acted true to form: as guardians and not as guides, overly cautious if not suspicious of our questions; deflecting and denigrating of our searches. We need remember that wherever our stories fall in the greater spectrum of such narratives, their telling, in and of itself, disturbs the status quo. In this light, time and retelling are on our side. And so whether I agree with their reasoning is wholly separate from understanding it; from making do with it; from working around it; from activating against it. I still wait for them to recognize the validity of my search, but this is no longer an impediment. With time, I imagine, this Truth will out.

There is much work to be done on both sides in this

regard. For to acknowledge another's quest positively is to extend a welcoming hand; to allow another their traveler's tale is to lend an ear; quite often this is more than enough: "I have a story to tell, but pray, tell me yours first." Here, there is grace. All the same, to acknowledge another's quest negatively is still, on some level, an allowance of its validity; an awareness of its strength. We should take both the positive and negative for what they are, understand their sources and derivations, attempt to change or avoid the detrimental aspects thereof to the best of our abilities, knowing that this might be temporary or indeed permanent, and from this find the energy to advance nonetheless. The road may be rocky, but at least we are not immobile, or frozen in lockstep, or sinking in place. Most importantly, we travel in good company.

In Arabic there is an expression that I hear at least a few dozen times a day: "*ahlan wa sahlan.*" Literally it means "[please find yourself among your] people and [your return journey is as on the] plain." Formerly stated to travelers whose journeys were often treacherous due to mountains, rocks, or sand, it remains an expression of welcome, an invitation to rest, as well as to rest assured. It is with such communal grace that I wish introduce this anthology of narratives. In following their ebb and flow in time and space, we are united in a communal voicing, a common grounding, revealing a bigger picture, inherently including our own stories that echo and resonate within and among them, no matter how much or how little we know or know to tell, and with the understanding that this selection is but a drop in a vast ocean, whose roar grows ever louder; a tidal wave on the swell. With each story told we stand a bit taller, our foothold a bit firmer, our place set a bit more fast; the narrative imbalance set more to rights.

I would only ask that we not stop here. We must find ourselves duty-bound to hear out as many such stories as we are able; to speak aloud ourselves, but more importantly to actively help others find their own voice in turn; not just in rarified niches and removed enclaves, but all along the full spectrum of societal strata, of media, and of our ability to express ourselves. I am proud and humbled to be included here, and I hope I have done honor to my fellow narrators with this introduction. As I reflect back on ten years spent "searching," I realize how much I have truly found. This requires taking a step back, and it is the compelling narratives of others as well as a reconfiguring of context that provide me with such perspective. Perseverance has paid off in ways I did not expect. I can honestly say that I have found much of what I have been seeking in listening to such voices; they set me steadfast. I am infinitely grateful to them for this. I hereby invite you to follow suit.

ahlan wa sahlan...

Daniel Drennan was born in Lebanon and adopted at two months. He grew up in Iran, Australia, and finally the United States, with four years lived in France. In 2004 he returned definitively to Lebanon, and has regained his nationality. Previously he was an assistant professor at the American University of Beirut. He founded the artists' collective Jamma Al-Yad, co-founded the adoptee collective Transracial Eyes, and is a collaborative member of Bada'el/Alternatives (Lebanon), which advocates for the right of children to know their origins. He writes using the pseudonym "Daniel Ibn Zayd."

Part 1

To Search or Not To Search,
Or,
Emerging from the Adoption Fog

Chapter 1

Sowing the Seeds for Emotional

Awakening and Eventual Reunion

By Rebecca Hawkes

"Do you think you will search for your birth mother someday?"

I was asked that question, in various forms, throughout my life. As a child, I came to understand that many people seemed to expect me to search (the age eighteen was sometimes mentioned as the magical number at which I might do so), but I also learned that my original birth certificate had been sealed. I believed that my original parents' identities had been obscured, legally and permanently. I had no idea how I would even begin to look for my biological family. I also learned that not everyone viewed searching favorably. Some clearly believed that reaching out to my biological family in any way would be an act of betrayal against my adoptive family—something that a "grateful" child would never do.

For many years, I answered the search question automatically, without much thought. In my childhood, the answer was, "Oh, yes, probably when I'm older." (In other words, that's a matter for a distant future that I can't even quite imagine yet.) In my teen years it became, "No. I have one mother already, and that's more than enough, thank you very much." Reunion wasn't something I contemplated often. It was too big and scary to approach, even in my thoughts.

The complexity of emotions for a pre-search adoptee is mind-boggling. The adoptee may have lived for years with denial and unprocessed grief over loss ("Why would I search? I'm just fine as I am.") Then there's the loyalty issue ("How will my adoptive family react if I search?"), and the big R, fear of rejection ("What if she doesn't want to be found? What if she refuses contact?").

The denial and unprocessed grief part of this equation loomed large for me. For most of my early life, I would have told you I was "just fine" with being adopted and had absolutely no adoption-related issues. But that would change.

My first "breakdown" happened in my early twenties. I was alone in my apartment and had been reading the novel, *Marya: A Life by Joyce Carol Oates*.

The book doesn't deal with a formal adoption, but the main character's father is dead and her mother has abandoned her. The ending of the book snuck past my defenses and touched on an adoptee nerve. Suddenly I had thrown the book across the room and was on the floor in tears. A wave of grief and loneliness came over me and completely knocked me flat. I kept repeating the phrase "she doesn't even know who I am" over and over again.

A second incident happened about a year later when I saw the movie, *The Joy Luck Club*. The scene at the end where one of the main characters returns to China to meet her two sisters completely undid me. I sat there in tears, unable to move from my seat as the credits rolled and other movie-watchers left the theater. And yet, I might not have even realized that my reaction had anything to do with adoption if the friend I was with hadn't asked me why the scene had affected me so intensely. Looking back now at my earlier years I can see lots of ways that my separation from my original family affected me throughout my life; I just didn't recognize the signs at the time. I would have described myself as happy, but now I see that much of that time I was actually closer to numb.

This was all pre-Internet, and I had no resources. I didn't even know enough to look for them. I had always been told that being adopted wasn't a big deal and that I was no different from children who were born into a family, so I had no way to make sense of all these feelings that I wasn't "supposed" to be feeling. I was completely alone.

These breakdown/breakthrough moments shifted me from thinking that I would never search for my biological family because I was "just fine without them." Obviously, I wasn't fine. It took a few more years before I really got up the nerve to search, but the seeds were sown during this period of emotional awakening.

I was still hesitant, however, to approach my adoptive mother with questions, and I couldn't bring myself to begin the search without her knowledge. But one day, the topic arose spontaneously in a conversation between us. She was very open to talking about my original family. In fact, she had been expecting the conversation for years but apparently believed that I needed to be the one to initiate it. And not only was she prepared to talk about it, she also had some surprising information.

There was a crack in the seal of my closed adoption; my adoptive mother knew the name of my biological mother. She couldn't remember how she got the information, but I've since come to understand that she probably saw it on the adoption decree. And the name wasn't all she had. One morning during my childhood she had opened up the paper to see my first mother's wedding announcement. She had cut it out and saved it, waiting for the day when I would ask about "my beginnings," as she put it.

I soon found myself sitting on the edge of my

childhood bed, my adoptive mother beside me, looking at that newspaper clipping. It included all of the little tidbits of biographical information that are typically involved in such write-ups. The bride had attended graduate school (as had I); she had lived in various places in the United States (as had I); she was a librarian (I was—and am—a lover of books). And then there was the photo! For the first time in my life, I saw my own face reflected back in the face of another. The resemblance was undeniable.

But I still didn't begin my search. Not yet. For a while, just having these little pieces of information was enough. I wasn't yet strong enough to handle the outcome I feared most: that she wouldn't want to know me or have contact with me.

I knew that the state I was born in had an adoption reunion registry, which functions as follows: if the parent registers and the adoptee registers, creating a match, the registry sends each party the other's identifying and contact information. I believe I first read about the registry in a magazine, years earlier before I was ready to do anything with the knowledge. A small window of possibility opened in my mind when I read about the registry, but I tucked the information away in the "someday" file. I hesitated for many years, in large part because I was afraid of the disappointment I knew I would experience if I discovered that she hadn't registered.

I was living on my own in a small, second floor

apartment when I finally decided to send my application to the registry. I can't say with certainty what had changed for me; it was simply time. I was 29 and recently married. (My husband was finishing up graduate school in another state but was set to join me soon to begin our life together.) I was working at a job that I expected to keep for a while. In other words, my life was relatively stable—enough so that I finally felt ready to take on the emotional risks of a search.

When the envelope arrived from the state, I knew immediately what was in it. I didn't make it into the apartment before I had the envelope opened. Sitting on the second floor landing outside the door to my apartment, I unfolded the single sheet of paper. And there it was: her name and address, and the date of her registration, a decade earlier. She had registered! She had been there waiting for me all along!

As it turned out, the address and phone number the registry sent were no longer accurate. But knowing that my mother had been open to being found, at least at one point, gave me the courage to take the next step. It required a bit of mild deception, but was surprisingly easy. I did it on my lunch break at work one day. Using the newspaper clipping that my adoptive mother had given me, I called the library where my original mother had been working at the time of her marriage. I said that I was trying to locate an old family friend who had worked at the library some years ago. I asked if there might be anybody there who could help me locate her. The friendly librarian who answered the phone said why yes, she knew her. No, she didn't live in town anymore, but her ex-mother-in-law did and would probably know where she was. I called the mother-in-law, and she answered right away. This time I said I was planning a surprise party for someone and trying to track down this person's old friends. Within minutes, I had my mother's current address.

I mailed her a note and included with it my own wedding announcement so that she would have the same biographical bits about me that I had about her. Then I went away for Thanksgiving and tried to put the matter out of my mind. When I returned to my apartment late on Sunday evening, my answering machine was blinking. Her voice! I played the message over and over.

I called her back the next day. I had a list of questions. This was before I had a cordless phone, so I sat on the wooden floor in my foyer. We talked for two mind-spinning hours. I heard about her life, her family, my father and their relationship, her pregnancy. She explained about her lack of options as an unmarried, teenage mother at that time in history, assuring me that it was never a matter of not wanting or loving me. She had held me in her heart through the years, always hoping I would contact her eventually.

Because of geographical circumstances, the first relatives I met in person were an aunt and uncle. I will never forget that night. I don't think I can adequately describe what a bizarre experience it was to have reached adulthood without ever having met a member of my immediate biological family, and then, suddenly, to see parts of myself reflected back in these people, who were strangers but not strangers at all. And it wasn't only the similarity of physical appearance, but also the unexpected little things, like gestures—the tendency to turn a hand a certain way when telling a story or a certain tilt of the head in photographs.

Initially, my relationship with my original mother consisted primarily of letters and emails. When we met in person for the first time about six months after our first phone call, we were immediately comfortable with each other, in large part because of all the correspondence we had exchanged. I also met my biological brother for the first time on that day. I will always remember being fascinated by his hands as we made tacos together in the kitchen—my hands, on the end of someone else's arms!

My mother and I have kept in touch ever since. Today, she is simply a part of my life. We communicate mostly through email and Facebook, and we see each other in person about once a year for a week or more. At first I struggled with loyalty issues, and I still do to some extent, but for the most part I have managed to let go of that, and to instead embrace the number two. I have two mothers; I love two mothers; I am loved by two mothers. This is my reality. It really is that simple.

I have now been in reunion with my mother for seventeen years. I have remained in contact with my brother and other extended family members. Recently, I also succeeded in establishing a relationship with my biological father—the final piece of the puzzle that is me. In these relationships I have discovered striking similarities of appearance, mannerisms, interests, personality, education, and even profession.

I have learned that reunion is not the end of the search for self; it is part of a lifelong process. I will always be adopted. I will probably always be engaged in the process of making sense of what it means to be a member of more than one family. But at least now I have some material to use. I know whose daughter I am: his and his, hers and hers. I am no longer thrown off balance by missing pieces.

I remember the profound loneliness I felt back before I had met any of the members of my biological family. I remember the confusion caused by the absence of knowledge. Reunion isn't always easy, but for me the time before reunion was worse. Much worse. I would not go back for anything.

Rebecca Hawkes is an adult adoptee in reunion and a mother of two daughters (one by birth and one by way of open foster-care adoption). She blogs at Sea Glass and Other Fragments and The Thriving Child. Additionally, she is a contributor at Adoption Voices Magazine and Lost Daughters. She is also a public speaker who has presented at various conferences, together with her adopted daughter's first mother, on the topic of open adoption from foster care. She lives in Western Massachusetts with her husband, her daughters, and a dog named Buddy.

Clarity Questions

1. The author confronts pre-search emotions such as, "I have no issues with having been adopted," numbness, and feeling "stuck." How did the author begin to sow her own personal seeds for emotional awakening?

2. Rebecca's adoptive mom waited for Rebecca to bring up the search. What do you think of this approach? Where did Rebecca get the idea that she shouldn't mention her original family in the first place? Are there any ways in which her adoptive mom could have fostered an environment that would have made it okay for Rebecca to ask and talk about her beginnings?

3. Can you be adopted and not search and be at peace? Is that denial or acceptance?

4. Rebecca's comfort level for initiating her search included having a stable support network, and reaching a state of emotional and professional stability before starting a search. Do you agree or disagree with this approach?

5. If you're in reunion, what were your questions for your original mom? If you're contemplating reunion, what questions would be on your list?

Chapter 2

A Mother Never Forgets

By Jeanne Nott

On Sept. 19, 1970, I saw my baby daughter for the first time through a small window in the door of the hospital nursery. That would be the last time I saw her for twenty-four years. At that time, there was no counseling for unwed mothers. You were told it was the best and only thing to do for your baby. When I told my mother I was pregnant, her first thought was to get me out of town so no one would find out. I was sent from my home in New Jersey to a home for unwed mothers in Omaha, Nebraska.

While I was at the maternity home, I learned about a little known practice of staying at a private home and helping out in exchange for room and board. I was sent to the home of a wealthy couple in Omaha. I had my own room and bath, and the evenings were the best time because I could be by myself. During the day I took care of the couple's three young children, cooked meals and cleaned the house. I often heard them on the phone referring to me as "their pregnant girl," and they told their friends that my husband was in the service overseas so I wouldn't be embarrassed.

At night, I would lie in bed and sometimes feel my baby move. I remember telling her (somehow, I always knew I was having a girl) that I wished I could keep her, but I didn't know how I could. My parents told me when they sent me away that they would disown me if I kept the baby. I had no place to go and no money for expenses. Even the home had no counselors. We were told that giving up the baby was the best and only choice. The baby needed a home with both a mother and father. After all, I could have other children and I would forget about the child I relinquished. But, I knew that I would never forget and I truly thought I was doing the best thing for my baby. I wanted her to have a loving home and I was told over and over that I could not provide that.

I never blamed my mom for sending me away. When I told my mother that I needed to talk to her, her first reply was "What have *you* done?" She concentrated on getting me out of town so no one would know and warned me never to tell anyone about it. I felt so much shame and guilt, especially when she told me, "If your grandmother finds out, it will kill her."

Shortly after I gave birth, I remember having a clipboard containing final papers for me to sign placed in front of me. I knew at that moment, that I needed to see my baby. I walked down the hall to the nursery and saw the sweetest little baby through the window. She looked exactly like my baby pictures.

I always hoped that one day my daughter would contact me, but of course, I never really thought it would happen. As much as I wanted to search for her, I never felt I had the right, and I was afraid to disrupt her life. Many times over the years, I would try to talk to my mother about the baby I had given up, but she would quickly change the subject. I thought it was because she was ashamed of me. Even though my mom and I remained close, it was one subject we never talked about.

My mother was like this and I guess I was not surprised by her actions. I remember when I started my period. I was young and my mother never talked to me about it, so when I started bleeding, I was scared. My mother handled the situation by tossing a box of Kotex on the bed and telling me there was a booklet inside that I should read.

People often ask me if I was angry with my mother for sending me away. I was not, but always wished she had been more open with me and that we could talk more about it. But, I was raised at a time when you were taught to "respect your elders," and I guess I felt like she was doing the right thing. It was hard being sent so far away from home and having to lie to just about everyone about where I was going. Even my younger brother and sister were told I was going to Nebraska to finish college there.

I never returned to New Jersey to live, even though all my family was back there. I think in my mind I felt like I was sent away, so no way would I ever go back. Mother and I stayed close, but she would never talk about what happened. It was as if she didn't talk about it, it never happened. I never forgot though, and for years it was difficult when I saw a baby or young child, wondering if it could be mine. When I had a hysterectomy at 30, I felt as though I was being punished for giving up my first child. It was a secret I held in my heart for a very long time.

In September 1994, I received a letter from the Nebraska Children's Home that simply stated, "We have a matter of extreme importance to discuss with you," and provided a phone number. That call changed my life.

A social worker told me my daughter was looking for me and asked if I wanted to be contacted. When I told her yes, she proceeded to give me what information she could. On October 3 (my birthday), I received my first letter. It was a long letter, and she included her college picture. Her name was Stacey. She told me all about her family.

I called my mother in New Jersey and told her that I had been put in touch with my daughter. She was very quiet. Again, I took her silence as shame. Finally, I told her that—and she began to cry. She said, "For 24 years, you thought I was ashamed of you. I was ashamed of myself for making you give up that baby."

When my mother finally told me that she regretted making me give up my child, we both broke down and wept. I wish she had lived long enough that she and my daughter could have met. I understand why my daughter has mixed feelings about my mother, because most people think I should have been angry with her. I really believe that my mom was a product of her generation and environment. I know she loved me and wanted the best for me. Although, I sometimes do blame myself for not being more independent and allowing her to make the decision for me.

With each ensuing letter and conversation, we learned more about each other. We decided to meet after Christmas.

In January 1995, I flew to Nebraska. It was the most wonderful weekend of my life. I told her what I had held in my heart for so many years. I told her that even though I had given her up for adoption, I always loved her. She hugged me and told me that she loved me, too.

Stacey had a wonderful relationship with her mother, dad and older brother. She was especially close to her mom and told me up front that she wasn't looking for another mother. But she hoped that we would become friends. She doesn't call me mom, but she is my daughter. I accept the fact that I am her biological mother, but the woman she calls mom is the woman who raised her. When she told me that she was not looking for another mother, I understood perfectly. When we are out together, I usually make it a point to introduce her as "my special friend" because she doesn't call me mom. My friends know the story and we look similar, so I think most people assume we are mother and daughter. A few times, she has introduced me to her friends as her "bio-mom," and I feel so proud.

Also, I think a part of me is very careful to keep that special bond with her. I am probably overly careful because I never want to lose her again, although she assures me that will never happen.

I did a lot of thinking while I was pregnant and far away from home. The one thing I was sure of was that I wanted my baby to have a good life with loving parents. When we finally met and we got to talk for hours, I knew that my wish had come true. I met her folks a few years later and then I really knew I made the right decision. She and I talk about everything and she knows the entire story. She knows that I was sent away by my mother, but also realizes that decision led to her being placed with a family that she loves and who truly loves her.

Twelve years ago, Stacey gave birth to a son. When he was two months old, I flew to Nebraska to see him. Stacey asked if I wanted to hold the baby. Without hesitation, I reached out. As I held him close, I remembered that day so many years ago when I stood by the nursery window and, for the first time in my life, I felt complete. She adopted a baby girl six years ago and is a wonderful mother.

After my daughter gave birth to her son, she asked me if I would mind if he called me by my first name instead of Grandma. It didn't bother me at all. I'm just so happy that I am in their lives. One time when we were all out together, a woman commented to my granddaughter, "Isn't it nice being out with your Grandma?" My granddaughter replied "Oh, Jeanne's not my Grandma. She is just my mom's biological parent."

Many years later, I told the birth father about the thirty-five-year-old daughter he never knew about. (Now, there's a whole other story!) He accepted the news with great joy and excitement and told his wife and children. We talked on the phone and I told him the entire story. What he said after that really touched my heart. He said, "I'm just so sorry that you had to go through that all alone."

During one of my recent visits back to my hometown, I stopped by to see his parents. He had shared the story with them after I told him. They welcomed me with open arms and I shared pictures of my daughter and her son. His mother told me something that haunts me to this day. She told me if I had come to them with my news, they would have opened their home to me and I could have raised my child with them. I couldn't even think of that because the decision was made and life turned out very differently. What I have to think of is my daughter and that she had a good life and is happy.

Originally published in shorter form in *The Denver Post*.

Jeanne Nott began entertaining audiences at age five and now, in her sixties, she performs stand-up comedy for seniors. She is an accomplished director and stage performer and was the recipient of an All-State Acting Award at the 2004 Colorado Community Theatre Coalition. Her children's play, *A House is Not a Home*, was presented at the Colorado Performing Arts Festival. Jeanne is also a Colorado Voices writer for The Denver Post. She and her husband, Dr. Paul Crumby, reside in Loveland, Colorado with their dog, "Rolo," who came from Animal Rescue of the Rockies.

Clarity Questions

1. What type of counseling, if any, do you think Jeanne ought to have received? What is your feeling on

how the author was treated as an expectant mother? Being sent away, being asked to sign relinquishment papers almost immediately after giving birth? Do you feel that she was treated ethically? Humanely?

2. This reunion story is written from the perspective of a first mom. What is your reaction to her feelings about reunion? Specifically, her gratefulness, her reluctance to upset the apple cart with her daughter?

3. What is your reaction to the fact that Jeanne's daughter adopted a child herself? How do you feel about the reality that the child calls her grandmother, "her mom's biological parent"?

4. Jeanne believed she had no other options; but came to find out that the baby's father's family would have been happy to help Jeanne raise her daughter. What was your reaction to this aspect of the story? Why do you think the author felt that she had no options, when in fact she did? How could counseling have helped this situation? How do you feel that Jeanne coped with this new information?

Chapter 3

Preparing for a Successful

Long-term Reunion

By Jessie Wagoner Voiers

I grew up knowing I was adopted at birth. I never remember this being revealed to me in some dramatic way. Adoption was a part of me, was a part of our family. It wasn't a secret or something that was whispered about. I arrived via a small airplane from the western part of our state at ten days old, and my parents fell madly in love with me. They told me my story of adoption regularly enough that it became a part of me. No surprises, just knowledge of how I came to be a part of this family.

As I grew up, I pretended my birth mother was a princess in a castle wondering where I was. I would ask my mom about her, and she would always say that they had not had the opportunity to meet her, but she just knew that my birth mom thought about me often and loved me. As I grew older and celebrated my birthday, I would ask my parents to tell me my adoption story. They would recall the call they received from the attorney, how hot it was the day I arrived, how nervous and excited they were and how much they loved me. I would again ask if my birth parents thought of me, and I was always reassured that they had no doubt that on this day and everyday my birth parents thought of me.

By the time I was fifteen, I needed to meet my birth family. I needed to know that they thought of me. I needed to know who I looked like and where that airplane that delivered me came from. I went to my parents and nervously asked them if we could try and find my birth family. Without hesitation my mom replied, "Of course we can, I have been waiting a long time to thank them for you." The feeling of relief that poured over me was indescribable. I never wanted my parents to feel like they weren't enough, or that I didn't love them, I just wanted to know more about me. Thankfully they understood that completely!

Before contacting the attorney and starting our search, my mom helped me create a list of what I wanted to know from my birth family. "What do you want this relationship to look like?" she asked. She wanted to make sure my expectations were realistic. She asked me tough questions like, "What will you do if they aren't ready to meet you?" and "What if you meet them and they aren't what you expect?" She also brought up some fun topics like, "What are the top ten things you think they should know about you?" and "Do you think the way you flare your nostrils is genetic? Let's see if they can do that!" Once our list was complete, we headed to the attorney's office.

As we sat in his office and explained that I wanted to meet my birth family, my stomach fluttered with nerves. He said it might take him a while to track everyone down. He acknowledged that he had contact information for my biological grandma but no one else. He would reach out to her and see what response he received. He patted me on the shoulder as I left and said, "Give me some time, these types of things can take a while." That was at 4:00 in the afternoon and at 9:00 that night, my biological grandma as well as my birth mom were on the phone with my mom. It didn't take much time at all!

That night we had our very first phone conversation. My mom did the majority of the talking for me as I was very nervous. She was tearful while talking to my birth mom. She thanked her for me and described how grateful she was to have me for a daughter. She asked my birth mom questions about her life, her hobbies, and what she would like this relationship to look like. After they chatted for a while, my mom handed over the phone to me. I remember saying hi and hearing a voice so similar to mine respond with a hello back. Before my birth mom could say much else, I blurted out that I didn't need her to be my mom, I had a really great mom, but I needed to know her and love her. Luckily, she totally understood that! As we hung up the phone that night we had already made plans to meet in person in just a few days.

In the time leading up to the reunion, my mom had been trying to prepare me. Her questions and lists were a way to try and help me navigate this new relationship. In hindsight, her preparation is what helped make our reunion so successful. She encouraged me to be open and honest with both her and my birth mom about my feelings. She also encouraged me to set clear boundaries. "Always say what you mean and mean what you say," was her motto. While we spent a great deal of time preparing for the first meeting, my mom had really been preparing me my whole life. By speaking so highly of my birth mom and being so open with me about my adoption in general, she gave me the confidence to develop the relationship. I could move forward without being fearful of hurting her. What a gift she had given me!

The day of our reunion finally came. Our first meeting actually occurred on Valentine's Day. I will never forget how amazing it was to open my front door and see my birth mom standing there. I had her nose and smile. Our laughs were the same! When she hugged me I felt like I had found a part of myself. We shared stories and pictures and tears and laughter. I could tell she was memorizing every part of me the way most women memorize their newborn infants.

I won't lie and say that over the past seventeen years our relationship has been flawless and perfect. Like all relationships, we have our bumps in the road. What has helped us navigate the rough patches is our commitment to being open and honest. Reunions are at times painful and at other times poetic. We have learned over time that our relationship doesn't have to look a certain way. We can develop a relationship that works for us and our families.

Now that seventeen years have passed, my birth mom has experienced a great deal of life with me. She attended my high school and college graduations, cheering loudly from the stands! She visited my mom while she was dying of cancer and was present and supportive at her funeral. We have shared our love of water and visited several lakes and aquatic parks to bask in the sun and swim. We both love to read and pass our newest favorites back and forth to each other. She now enjoys the role of "Grandma Hottie" to my son and took part in my wedding. Most of all she is my friend! A friend I love, a friend I respect, and a friend I cannot imagine living without.

Jessie Wagoner Voiers is an adult adoptee in reunion and also mom to six children (one through an open domestic adoption and five bonus children gifted to her upon marriage). She writes about blending families, adoption, parenting, and how to find the humor in the everyday on her blog Then I Laughed.   Additionally, Jessie is an advocate for children and families affected by Fetal Alcohol Syndrome. Connect with Jessie on twitter @mamalaughsagain.

Clarity Questions

1. What are your thoughts on the way in which Jessie's adoptive mom approached the reunion?

2. Similar to Jeanne Nott's daughter, adoptee Jessie felt it necessary to underscore that she's not looking for another mom. To what do you attribute this statement? How do you feel about this? It is possible to have a first mom and an adoptive mom, simply two moms?

3. When navigating reunion as a teenager, Jessie gathered a lot of confidence when her adoptive mom had her prepare questions ahead of time. What other ideas do you have as to how an adoptee can prepare for reunion?

Chapter 4

Adoption Fog and

Deciding Not to Search

A Conversation with Laura Dennis and Corie Skolnick

Laura—We just had three articles, two from adoptees and one from a first mom. These three stories had relatively happy endings. Not all of them are like that, and the fear of rejection can be huge. Can you talk a little more about why people are so resistant to reunion?

Corie—This is a tough subject for some.

I can tell you what I've witnessed as a clinician, and I can tell you what my suppositions are, but, remember, only the individual in question can tell you themselves why they are resistant to reunion, and many will not care to even ponder the notion of reunion let alone analyze their resistance to it. Nobody is saying that the following is accurate in describing any particular individual's experience.

Laura—Okay, tell me more about resistance from your point-of-view then.

Corie—First let me say that human beings for the most part are resistant to change of any kind. Physiologically, as living organisms, we are programmed to survive, and at the biological level, changing anything about our experience, even seemingly insignificant things, can be somewhat taxing–organically speaking.

Medical science has demonstrated that change is stressful. This is true for both kinds of changes, positive and negative. When things change, no matter the valence, we go on high alert. Our bodies react significantly by amping up the production of hormones that will give us an edge if we need to flee danger, or fight off an attacker, or perceived attacker, or if we need to perform some function that isn't ordinary for us. Those chemicals are fabulous in the short-term, but, destructive at the organic level over prolonged or repeated exposure.

So, it's easy to see why, at this mindless, unconscious level, we will see the organism avoid change. Less change equals less stress. Our primitive wiring in effect makes us seek out the status quo. That kind of resistance is physiological and adaptive and utterly pre-conscious.

Laura—This is actually helpful insight for me, because when I look at it this way, I can see that some people are more adaptable, they are more able handle change in general. I personally have such a difficult time relating to the notion of being adopted, and not being curious. I just can't fathom how one would not wonder. Would not want, not *need*, to know the real story, straight from the horse's mouth, so to speak.

But like you say, most people resist change. And search and reunion, at their core, require change. When it comes to an adopted person who resists reunion, they may be change- adverse in other areas of their lives, as well. It may be a symptom to a general reluctance to create change anywhere, not necessarily only when it comes to adoption.

Clearing out the adoption fog equals change, something we are hard-wired to resist. And for those who are in the midst of "being found," well, they're thrust into dealing with reunion change, whether they're ready or not.

The fog, therefore, is protective, a coping mechanism. This makes perfect sense as to why certain life changes can often push a person out of the fog. For example, turning 18 and having their original birth records unsealed. Or when adoptees have children of their own. Emerging from the fog can happen when an adoptee faces a health crisis, creating an absolute medical necessity to discover one's medical history. Can you talk a little more about how this resistance to change relates to adoption fog, specifically in adoptees who don't want to search?

Corie—"Adoption fog" describes a state that is personally emotional, mental, physical and psychological. At a systemic level, the "fog" extends to the entire social system that revolves around a child that is not being raised by its biological parents. "Adoption fog" is REALLY complex and entirely subjective.

No two adoptees will experience "adoption fog" in exactly the same way. No family system will maneuver the fog in the same way. The complexity of such a phenomenon requires a lot more research and study and as more and more people within the adoption community "come out" I hope we see a dedicated professional interest in this topic.

For the purpose of this discussion though, when you talk about "adoption fog" as it pertains to adoptees who don't want to search, I'm going to assume that you are talking about adoptees who have not yet come to terms with the reality of their feelings. In the fog, everything is "fine, fine, fine." In the fog, the denial of any dreaded reality, i.e. typically, "my mother didn't want me" may not be entirely possible, but the denial of the adoptee's feelings about that reality are. This denial often gets expressed as resistance to the notion of reunion, or even rejection of the birth parents altogether. "I don't care about her. (Them.) I don't need to know anything about her. (Them.)"

Denial is the name of the game in the fog.

Nobody has any bad feelings as long as the fog is maintained. The adoptee has no anger, no fear, no resentment... none that can be seen in the fog anyway. You put this very well in terms of your own experience. It sounds like the thing that dispelled the fog in your case was your overwhelming curiosity about the truth of your life's experiences. All of them.

But, again, each person's fog is their own.

What does or doesn't bring a person out of the fog and into a "need to know" that activates a search and reunion will be unique to them. It's important to remember that the fog is protective. The who, how and why someone needs to be protected from reunion and all the feelings about it is going to be completely idiosyncratic, even within the same family.

An adoptee might be certain that their adoptive parents need to be protected from their curiosity to find their birth parents and they may be pre-supposing that a reunion represents catastrophe for their entire family. At the very same time, adoptive parents might be encouraging the fog because they believe that they are protecting the adoptee from a search that might result in a bad outcome.

Laura—It's true, some (not all) adoptive parents resist their adoptee's search and reunion. Whether it's passive aggressive or outright, their reluctance to show support hinders the adoptee's ability to cope with and process their own feelings.

My adoptive mom was in fact quite supportive and even helped me with my search to find my first mom. Even so, I felt like, Hey you had 18 years to get comfortable with this, you're on your own. My search is about my emotions, my reactions. I had so much going on inside me personally, I had little left over to help her. And I think that's okay. I think search should be about the adoptee. Why is it do you think there's push back from adoptive parents?

Corie—The adoptive parents that I've known who actively or passively resisted their kid's reunion were by and large either uninformed or somehow damaged. Not all parents are psychologically sophisticated, so of course that's true for adoptive parents too. What I mean by this is that a parent's general ignorance about child development and/or their own lack of personal autonomy can promote enormous insecurity when the adoptee hits the normal adolescent stage of identity formation.

Adolescence is a tough developmental stage in

"ideal" family circumstances, but adoptees are coping with issues that complicate the process of identity formation. In short, just when a kid is psychologically programmed to differentiate from their parents and become an individual, they get slammed hard with the truth of their origins. They don't really know who they are differentiating from. And they do need to know.

If an adoptive parent doesn't understand that an adoptee's curiosity "to know" is completely normal and to be expected, they can take it personally and feel rejected or become fearful that they will lose their "child." Imagine how much worse that insecurity is going to be if the parent never achieved their own healthy personal autonomy.

Adults that fail to individuate will often experience this normal developmental stage in their kids as hostility, or, worse, adoptive parents sometimes perceive this stage in terms of a lack of gratitude (for being "rescued") If the situation is further complicated by a history of infertility and the adoptive parents never resolved their grief over that, it's quite common for all those feelings of insecurity and fear and anger to be magnified. I've heard many adoptees express anger that they had been pressured to display gratitude for their adoptions.

It takes a really healthy and informed parent to encourage a kid's autonomous identity formation. It takes a healthy adult to help a child manage extreme feelings, especially when a child expresses a need to find their original family members and to be reunited with them.

Laura—You mentioned something about "resistance being worn down," that "putting a desire for reunion into action sometimes takes years, even decades." Can you talk more about navigating through and out of the adoption fog?

Corie—People change over time. I know of more than a few cases wherein an adoptee was once upon a time very opposed to the notion of finding their birth parents. As circumstances change, sometimes just with maturity, people come out of the fog. For more than a few people I've worked with, the fog evaporated when they became a parent. It's not uncommon for an adoptee to have a "sudden" urge to find their birth parents on behalf of their own children when they will tell you that they truly experienced zero curiosity prior to becoming a parent.

When a birth parent is resistant to reunion with their relinquished child who has become an adult, I'm suspicious that there's still some shame operating on them that makes them want to maintain secrecy and resist reunion. And, of course, not everyone is capable of rejecting the attitudes of the people around them who might still think of them as "bad" or "sinful." Birth mothers deserve punishment in some quarters and especially in very fundamentally religious groups the deprivation of knowing their child seems a reasonable penance for their sin. That's harsh and sad, but not unheard of.

When extended family members, like your own first brother who resists contact with you, have resistance to reunion, it makes me wonder why their life is so puny that they can't make room for another person to know and maybe even love. It really speaks of a lack of maturity possibly and I have to say, even though I know it hurts you, I think that's his problem. Try not to take that on. It says nothing about you at all but it does say something about him.

I think I told you that it took my father's half-brother almost ten years to finally tell the third brother about my dad's very existence, and then to actually facilitate a meeting. [Editor's note: read more about it in Corie's article later in this book, called "Reunion Once Removed."]

And, remember, ALL families are not big happy gangs of mutually accepting members. In fact, that's kind of the exception, not the norm. Plenty of people who were raised with their biological sibs, just plain don't have the capacity to connect. Lots of people are estranged from their families of origin. It's not always about adoption. Then again, sometimes people have a change of heart for any number of reasons. If you don't close the door, you might get surprised. It's the never say never rule.

So, to close, let me say that we barely touched the

surface of this topic. A whole book could be written on the subject of resistance to reunion. But, if I had to sum it up in one word, I would say... fear. I'll leave it for the triad members to identify for themselves what might be fearsome about searching for, finding and adding a new member to their family.

Corie Skolnick is the author of *Orfan*, a novel. She is a licensed California Marriage and Family Therapist and has been an adjunct faculty member in the Psychology Departments of both California State University, Northridge (CSUN) and Moorpark College.

The Comparative Literature Program at San Diego State University selected Corie and *Orfan* for the prestigious Hugh C. Hyde Living Writers Series in the Spring of 2012, and Orfan was nominated for the 2012-2013 Freshman Common Reading Selection at Cal State University, Northridge.

Her second novel, *America's Most Eligible* will be published by MVP/MVR in 2014.

Clarity Questions

1. What are your personal views on adoption fog? Do you agree that each person's fog is their own?

2. Does the society at large manifest a type of fog about adoption? Is the topic still taboo? Is this changing?

3. Corie says, "It takes a really healthy and informed parent to encourage a kid's autonomous identity formation." How can this apply to adoptive parents? How can adoptees—in childhood and adulthood, develop this autonomous identity?

Part 2

Closed vs. Open Adoption:

History and Logistics,

Or,

'DNA Doesn't Lie'

Chapter 5

Open and Closed Adoptions, How They Got That Way

By Addison Cooper

When I train prospective foster and adoptive parents about openness in adoption, I ask them whether they think adoptions in the United States have historically been open or closed. Most of them haven't looked ahead in the PowerPoint handouts, and so they answer with what they honestly think. A large majority believe that adoptions have always generally been closed, and most haven't considered openness for their own desired adoption. It's not that they want a closed adoption— they just haven't asked themselves the question of openness.

The thing is, adoptions haven't been historically closed. If you're willing to consider openness as a continuum, they've been historically open. At the very least, the secrecy that seems so prevalent in American adoptions is far newer than most prospective adoptive parents initially think.

Adoption has not always been under the scope of public law. At times, adoption was a non-formalized arrangement, but if a child was being raised by a person other than their biological parent, the child and the public knew about it.

I've recently come to love the *Anne of Green Gables* books by L.M. Montgomery. In the first book, pre-teen orphan Anne is adopted by siblings Matthew and Marilla Cuthbert. Everyone in Avonlea knew that Matthew and Marilla were not the biological parents of Anne. And public knowledge was the norm for as far back as I can see.

Public knowledge wasn't without problems, though. Montgomery writes about the uncertainty that the Cuthberts' neighbors felt at their choice to care for an orphan. Busybody neighbor Mrs. Rachel Lynde was quick to express her belief that orphans were somehow less safe, not as good as, and less natural than a child born to a family. Anne experienced prejudice based on her status as an orphan.

While Anne is fictional, the judgments she faced were grounded in reality. Many children who were adopted had single mothers. A century ago in the United States, society viewed single mothers as having done something wrong, and they also attributed the perceived "wrong" of the mother to the character of the child. Children born outside of marriage were called "illegitimate"—which is the same word used to describe a monarch who attains his position through unorthodox and therefore invalid means. Society seems to have expected little good from orphans, and treated them poorly.

Because the information was public record, there was no protection offered to buffer the children from prejudice. Minnesota was the first state to change this. In 1917, Minnesota enacted a law which kept adoption records confidential from the public. There was no intention to keep the adoption records confidential from the parties in the adoption. The law made it so that a nosy neighbor couldn't poke into a child's record, but the law was not intended to make the child's record inaccessible to the child, the adoptive parents, or the birth parents.

The confidentiality was intended to protect the children from undue scrutiny, but benefits were also found by adoptive and birth parents. Adoptive parents could hide the fact that their family was formed through adoption, perhaps denying or hiding the infertility or difficult family circumstances which brought about the adoption. Birth parents—especially birth mothers—could be protected from public judgment for having a child out of wedlock. So confidentiality morphed into secrecy.

I find it helpful to differentiate between confidentiality and secrecy. They may be similar, but they are different in degree and implication. A person practicing confidentiality views their story as their property which they can share at will, but which they have the right to not share. A person oppressed by secrecy either views their story as shameful and unsharable, or has had their story withheld from them by someone else. Children are adopted. Adults make laws. And adults opted for secrecy instead of confidentiality. By the end of the Second World War, adoption records were largely sealed. Adoptees would join nosy neighbors in being denied access to the adoptee's birth certificate. No contact, no information.

Most prospective adoptive parents say that they think this has been the historical norm. But it only came into prominence in the 1950's, and was challenged almost immediately. In the 1970's, Florence Fisher founded the Adoptee Liberty Movement Association. The ALMA asserts that adoptees have the right to their own story. They fought for adoptees to have access to their original birth certificates, and coined the term "birth parent" to give a name to those people whose identities were locked away and inaccessible, while still acknowledging the important role and position of adoptive parents.

Secrecy in adoption today is rooted in beliefs which seem questionable. While some birth parents may not want to be found, the law treats adoption as though none of them do. While some adoptees would not choose to find out their full history, the law makes that choice for many adoptees regardless of what they want. Some adoptive parents might choose to let fear close off any possibility of openness, but in many cases, the law makes that decision uniformly. The law opts for secrecy where confidentiality would be more appropriate. In doing so, it seems to portray adoption as shameful, and to suggest that no birth parents want to be found, all adoptive parents want to avoid birth parents, and no adoptees should have the right to have their questions answered.

A growing Internet community stands to counter the thoughts behind the laws of secrecy. Birth parents with closed adoptions voice their grief. Birth parents with open adoptions express the difficulty inherent in complex and complicated relationships but also serve as a testament to the fact that the relationships can be meaningful and healthy. Adoptive parents with open adoptions share about the positive experiences of openness. Questions are answered, relationships maintained, and new, inclusive families are formed. Adult adoptees blog about the pain of closed relationships or, alternatively, the difficult but desired journey of reunification. Openness involves many strong emotions, and some of them are unpleasant. But overall, the vocal adoption community on the Internet seems to see openness as a good thing. Perhaps like running a marathon—it's difficult, it hurts, there's a sense of fulfillment, perhaps a sense of accomplishment, occasionally injuries, and lots of community. But above all, it's the right of the adoptee to run the marathon, to take the journey, to choose whether they want openness in their adoption.

In some states, adoptees have access to their birth records. In other states, the records are sealed. Adoptees in sealed states might not know where they were born, whether they have siblings, or even what their name was at birth. Perhaps the records stay sealed because there is a prevailing thought that "things have always been this way." But it's just not true.

In this collection, you'll read the words, journeys, and hearts of many who have been touched by adoption. Some will relate positive experiences; some will relate negative experiences. Most will relate mixed experiences. But the choice to journey through openness is theirs to take, if they want. It has to be. It's their right.

Addison Cooper, LCSW runs the adoption movie review website, Adoption at the Movies. He is a foster care adoption supervisor in Southern California. Find him on Facebook at Adoption at the Movies.

Clarity Questions

1. Adoptions in the United States were not always closed, did not always involve no contact and sealed records. Do you feel that laws have kept pace with society? Is there still shame and stigma associated with single motherhood? Why do you think these laws remain in place?

2. Many people are not aware of the reality that adoptees who do not have access to their Original Birth Records are essentially second class citizens, meaning they cannot get security clearances, passports, and an accurate medical history. What can be done to change the real impact that closed records have on adoptees lives?

Chapter 6

We Didn't Want Reunion

So We Chose Openness Instead

By Lori Holden

I once wrote a series about how my then seven-year-old daughter reunited with her birth dad. However, "*re*united" was not quite an accurate term, since they had never been *united* in the first place. Some people thought my husband and I were crazy to make this connection happen when we could have easily kept it unmanifested. But we'd seen over the course of our daughter's life the benefits of contact with her birth mother. We wanted our daughter to have access to all the parts of herself so that she would have the best shot at integrating her identity— the pieces that come from her biology and the pieces that come from her biography.

So when some complicated issues unknotted that year, we spent several months getting to know Tessa's birth dad, first by email, then through a meeting of the grownups, then a talk with Tessa, and finally a meeting with Joe and his wife and kids. While the initial meetings were successful, exhilarating even, difficulties arose as time passed. Tessa felt an uncomfortable push-pull between her two parts, and at times it was just too much for her. At one point she threw down photos of her birth family members, adamant that she no longer wanted to have two families. That time period was excruciating for us all. We did not react by throwing out the proverbial bathwater and baby—shutting down the relationships. Instead we reflected, talked, brought hidden emotions to the surface, and were then able to then deal with them mindfully.*

Today we remain in contact with both of Tessa's birth parents, as well as her birth siblings and the rest of her birth clans—birth grandparents, aunts and uncles. We keep Joe posted on school functions, volleyball games, and birthday celebrations, so that he and his family know they are welcome to join us as extended (and honored) family members.

But, truth be told, way back when we started out on this adoption journey, our vision was all about *avoiding* reunion. But not in the way you may think.

A Confession

Back during Adoption School (a three-day class required by our agency), when being a mom was just a theoretical concept, I did not embrace open adoption because the social workers said it was proving to be better for the child than shame and secrecy. I did not choose it out of gratitude to the theoretical woman who would eventually make me a mother.

I chose open adoption for selfish reasons. I looked ahead to the time my future hypothetical children would turn 18 and *I* didn't want to go through the jealousy and insecurity *I* would feel if and when they decided to wonder, to seek, to meet their birth parents.

That, I thought, would gut me. I thought I would feel betrayed. I worried I would think my children disloyal. I had grown up with friends in closed adoptions who were afraid to search for, to even wonder about their birth parents, for fear of appearing disloyal to the parents who raised them. I have since read adoption reunion memoirs by authors such as Laura Dennis and Anne Bauer, and I've confirmed that many adoptive mothers in closed adoptions often feel miserably insecure if and when their children search for their "real" mom.

In a flash, things shifted. During Adoption School, when we were formulating our vision for how future family might look and function, I wondered how reunion from a closed position would feel for my future hypothetical children, being split between their love for their parents and their curiosity about their birth parents. Would they be afraid to even wonder about, much less search for and meet their birth parents, because of the ensuing feelings of disloyalty for my husband and me?

How could I do that to my future hypothetical children, tear them in two?

I think it's natural to wonder. I would, had I been adopted. This doesn't mean all will wonder, for I've certainly met many closed-era adoptees who have expressed no desire to explore their roots.

But if my future hypothetical children turned out to have the curiosity that I do, I didn't want them to have to mend an 18+ year split. I thought that reunion at the young-adult stage of life would be incredibly complicated because of all that was missed. How would you forge a relationship with a stranger who was once and always so intimately integral to your very being?

It seems to me that search and reunion after a lifetime of separation would be very difficult to navigate—not just the relationship, but the feelings that go with establishing it. If I could prevent my future hypothetical children from having to go through search and reunion, I resolved that day during Adoption School, I would do so.

Some of the misery that closed-era adoptive moms feel when their grown child searches may stem from the Either/Or construct we have traditionally held about adoption, something I talk a lot about in my book, *An*

Open-Hearted Way to Open Adoption. There is a mindset that a person can have only one mother and one father. If there happens to be another in existence, the idea of him/her must be suppressed because it doesn't fit the construct. This duality pits one set of parents against the other. It legitimizes one while negating the other. Two mothers become a threat to each other, in competition. Only one can win, meaning only one can be in the picture.

And the baby, the child, the teen, the adopted adult, is split.

An Alternative

In listening to adoptee friends online, as well as my own children, I have come to embrace an alternative: Both/And thinking. Neither Crystal nor I are fake moms. We are both real, with valid contributions to the daughter we both claim. And, as more than one adoptee has pointed out, we fully expect that a parent can love more than one child. We hold high the Both/And mindset when considering parent-child relationships. Why can't we make the not-so-big shift to also hold a Both/And mindset with child-parent relationships?

We can! When adoptive parents know it's an option and consciously choose that option, the Both/And mindset is just as possible as—and less destructive than—the Either/Or mindset. People just need to know why and how to "adopt" this alternative way of thinking.

What about MY relationship with Tessa's birth

parents? Sure, I've helped facilitate Tessa's relationships, but what about my own? I'm incredibly fortunate that Crystal and I genuinely like each other and thus have a friendship independent of our daughter. Same with Joe. Over time we have become friends in our own right. Among us we extend respect trust and thoughtfulness, the way we do with others whom we value and who are important to us.

I should add that another key ingredient is that we *decided* to make things work. I would caution that you can't expect everything to happen on its own because without intention, you're taking the risk that it won't happen at all. Maintaining open adoption relationships does take effort at times—just like any relationship does. Being conscious, mindful and deliberate in these open adoption relationships has helped us keep them healthy and vibrant and enriching.

Reunion: Bringing People Together, Not Tearing Anyone Apart

One image I have for adoption reunion is a zipper. You pull on the tab to merge two into one. When birth parents and the person they created live in an open adoption from the beginning—or, in the case of Joe, from *near* the beginning—the spread between the zipper's teeth isn't so wide to make the closing the gap tough. To run with the metaphor, the surrounding fabric (adoptive parents) is also not overly stressed as the two sides interconnect. Reunion remains solely about bringing people together—not tearing anyone apart.

In our open adoption, reunion isn't a process we navigated once with big, dramatic results. Instead, it's something we do often. The frequency somewhat mitigates the intensity. We occasionally have drama, but the peaks and valleys have been no more, no less, than other less emotionally charged relationships.

I know it's too early in the history of open adoptions to tell, but it's my expectation that ethically-done adoptions with open-hearted participants will mean less reunion drama for adoptive families in the future. It will also mean that adopted people will have an easier time integrating all the parts of themselves. What's required is for adoptive parents see union/reunion from their child's point of view.

Which is why books like this filled with stories like these are so important.

To read this reunion series, visit
http://bit.ly/openadoptionreunionstories.

Lori Holden writes regularly at LavendarLuz.com about parenting and living mindfully and is a columnist at *The Huffington Post* and at the *Denver Post*'s moms site.

She is the author of *The Open-Hearted Way to Open Adoption: Helping Your Child Grow Up Whole*, written with her daughter's birth mom and after listening to adult adoptees and first parents tell of their varied experiences. She lives in Denver with her husband and two tweens and speaks to adoption agencies and their clients about openness in adoption and giving equal access for all citizens to original birth records. She has been known to practice the Both/And mindset when it comes to red wine and dark chocolate.

Clarity Questions

1. The author admits that she entered "Adoption School" with a preconceived notion of how *she* would handle a reunion, but learned to shift her focus to how her child might want to integrate her birth and adoptive families. How can adoptive parents be encouraged to make such a shift?

2. Which is better, in your opinion for the adoptee? Closed adoption secrecy, or open adoption messiness?

Chapter 7

How DNA Testing is Changing the World for Adoptees

By Richard Hill

Many adoptees have natural questions about our first families, our ethnicity, and our medical history. Yet in all but a few states, we are denied access to our original birth certificates.

Now Our Own DNA Can Get Around All the Secrecy

In the last few years a series of innovative DNA tests—in a field known as *genetic genealogy*—have been used by adoptees to overcome lies, secrecy, and sealed records to learn the truth about our own beginnings and reunite with biological families.

Besides being far more powerful, these direct-to-consumer tests are reasonably priced and can be taken in the privacy of your home. You simply choose the test you want, place the order online, and wait for the home test kit to arrive in the mail. Sampling is painless, involving either the gentle scraping of cells inside your cheek or the collection of saliva in a tube.

Within weeks, you can now discover amazing new facts about your ethnicity and your inherited health risks. If your biological parents had a few generations of American roots, you will almost certainly discover previously unknown cousins from your biological family tree.

From this new information you can inch your way down the branches of that tree and finally have a chance of identifying birth parents and siblings.

More Good News

Adoptee pioneers, such as this author, had to figure all this out on our own. But now a number of adoptees, search angels and genetic genealogists have joined forces to create an online community that educates and supports adoptees. We have even developed online tools to help you advance more quickly from your DNA data to contact with living, breathing relatives. And all the information and advice is free. See Important Resources at the end of this article.

Comparisons Are the Keys

You can gain all this knowledge by testing the DNA of just one person—yourself. All the apparent "magic" comes from comparing your DNA to genetic data already stored in various databases.

Finding biological relatives results from directly comparing your DNA to all the individuals who took the same type of test. More than a half million people are now in these databases and thousands more are taking these tests every week. So the number and closeness of your matches will tend to increase over time.

Estimating your ethnicity comes from comparing your DNA to dozens of scientifically accepted population studies. One company is now achieving even more specific results through the clever use of self-reported origins of people in their database.

Learning where you stand on genetically influenced health issues results from checking your DNA in certain locations that have known medical associations. Your risk for a particular condition, such as heart disease, Alzheimer's, or a particular form of cancer, may be higher or lower than average. Then there is your carrier status for diseases you could pass on to your children and your likely response to certain drugs.

Now you can capture all this genetic health knowledge without knowing the medical history of your parents.

Improvements in Relationship Testing

When an adoptee finds a biological family member, there is sometimes a need for confirmation. For decades DNA paternity testing has provided unequivocal Yes/No answers to suspected parent-child relationships. Now even those tests are usually done through home test kits.

But what if the biological parent is deceased or otherwise unavailable for testing? That simple paternity test technology has sometimes been applied to test other relationships. Yet these so-called "sibling" or "kinship" tests can only produce statistical guesses that are frequently inconclusive and sometimes misleading.

Fortunately, some of the newest genetic genealogy tests check such large amounts of people's DNA that they can confirm a wide variety of suspected relationships, including full siblings, half siblings, aunts and uncles, grandchildren, and even first or second cousins.

Your DNA Testing Options

There are three main categories of DNA tests in genetic genealogy. Here's a brief summary of each type and how it's used by adoptees:

1. Y-DNA Testing

This is for men only, because only we have a Y-chromosome. The markers on that chromosome pass down virtually unchanged from father to son, generation after generation. In Western culture surnames usually follow the same path. So barring a name change, adoption, or some other "non-paternity event" in the line, the men we match most closely should have the same surname as our biological father.

According to Family Tree DNA, adopted men taking the company's Y-DNA test are learning biological surnames about 40% of the time. Additional successes will occur as more men join their already huge Y-DNA database. You should test a minimum of 37 markers.

Y-DNA testing will also define your paternal line haplogroup. This will tell you in what parts of the world your direct paternal line ancestors lived tens of thousands of year ago.

2. Mitochondrial DNA Testing

Everyone has mitochondrial DNA (mtDNA), but only women pass it on. Since it passes down the female line, we might imagine that it could identify our birth mother. Unfortunately, the matches we get most likely reflect common ancestors from hundreds or even thousands of years ago. Plus, the surnames usually change every generation down the maternal line. So mtDNA testing rarely provides useful information about your recent family tree.

The test will define your maternal haplogroup, most precisely with the Full Mitochondrial Sequence test at Family Tree DNA. Certain results are a direct confirmation of Native American ancestry in the maternal line. Yet the only thing most people are likely to learn is where in the world your direct maternal line ancestors lived in ancient times.

3. Autosomal DNA Testing

The most recent breakthrough for adoptees is a new form of autosomal test that checks at least 700,000 locations on your genome. These are the tests that are so powerful for confirming close relationships.

Furthermore, just by testing themselves, both men and women can find biological cousins from any branch of their family trees. This is where adoptees should be investing most of their time and money.

While a few adoptees taking these tests have discovered an immediate match with a biological sibling, that is extremely rare. More typically, your first matches will be distant cousins of varying degrees. But even those matches can be fascinating to people who never knew a biological relative. What's more, these matches are potentially quite useful for discovering truths and finding closer relatives.

A third cousin designation, for example, says that you and your match have some great-great grandparents in common. Some of the people you match will be genealogists with extensive family trees and your task will be to find a branch that extends forward from the common ancestors to the time and place of your birth.

There are so many family trees and genealogy

resources online today that much, if not all, of this research can be done from the comfort of your home.

Currently, only three companies offer this type of test:

Family Tree DNA.com, the leader in the genetic genealogy field, offers a test called Family Finder. They are also the recommended lab for Y-DNA and mtDNA testing.

23 and Me has just one test, which includes a matching feature called DNA Relatives. This is the only test of the three that also includes a report on your genetic health traits.

Ancestry.com has recently entered the field with a test called AncestryDNA.

As an adoptee, you should take the first two tests for sure and add the third one if you can afford it. Fishing in multiple ponds is the fastest way to find the breakthrough matches that can help you put all the pieces together.

Ethnicity Reports Included

All three of these autosomal tests do some form of bio-geographical analysis. This provides a percentage breakdown of your overall ethnic ancestry. The Family Finder report is called "Population Finder." The 23andMe report is called "Ancestry Composition."

The ethnicity estimate included with the AncestryDNA test was initially flawed but has now been fixed.

Some Limitations

The people with the greatest chance of successfully finding their first families are those who happen to have deep roots in Colonial America. That's because they will have hundreds of cousins in the databases and many of those relatives are likely to have extensive family trees.

Those born to recent immigrants—and adoptees from countries outside the U.S.—are unlikely to discover their biological families any time soon through DNA testing. That's because most of their distant cousins are outside the U.S. and the sample sizes from abroad are still too small.

Even though they cannot expect to see a lot of cousin matches, these adoptees can still learn about their ethnic backgrounds and inherited medical issues. Those benefits alone may be enough to justify the relatively small cost of these new DNA tests.

A Plea for Parents

If you or someone in your family once gave up a child for adoption, please consider taking at least one of the new autosomal DNA tests. There's a small chance that you could get an immediate match with the adoptee that's been looking for you. At a minimum, you would be preserving your genetic markers and making it much easier for that child (or grandchild) to identify her first family someday.

Important Resources

The world of genetic genealogy can be confusing and very little has been written about the specific applications for adoptees. In addition to following the previous links in this article, you need to check out the following resources that DO cover this subject extensively:

DNA-Testing-Adviser. This is the website created and maintained by the author of this article, who found his first family through DNA testing. You can learn more about the different DNA tests and the strengths and weaknesses of the different testing labs. There's even a Feedback Form for asking individual questions. This is the site to visit *before* you order any tests.

Adoption DNA (a Yahoo Group). This is the Yahoo Group for adoptees and search angels to get methodologies, tips and tools for analyzing DNA results and finding families. It is also the ongoing discussion forum you should join *after* you get your results.

Finding Family: My Search for Roots and the Secrets in My DNA. This is the highly acclaimed book where Richard Hill tells his personal story: accidentally discovering he was adopted and his detective-like search for roots that spanned more than thirty years. This includes the details of the DNA tests that helped him find his first family even though both parents were deceased and no one else had known of their secret relationship.

Richard Hill is the author of *Finding Family: My Search for Roots and the Secrets in My DNA*. A decades-long search for his biological family introduced Richard to DNA testing. Motivated to share his success secrets and tips with other adoptees and genealogists, he created his web site, DNA-Testing-Adviser.com.

As the unifying expert bridging the fields of genetic genealogy and adoption search, he has become the go-to person for adoptees, genealogists, and others seeking to find lost relatives or confirm suspected relationships. His groundbreaking use of genetic genealogy tests was featured on the front page of *The Wall Street Journal*.

Clarity Questions

1. How important is your medical history to you? Has this changed over the years—with any health scares, or, if you're a biological parent, the birth of your own non-adopted children?

2. How important is it for adoptees to have access to this information?

3. Would you like to know your biological ethnicity? Do you feel like you have acquired a cultural ethnicity from your adopted family? Would you be surprised, upset, or simply intrigued if these two ethnicities proved to be quite different?

4. What would it be like to correspond with or meet a biological relative, even if he or she were only a distant cousin?

Chapter 8

Your Story: Your Birthright

By Lynn Grubb

Many times when adoptees are thinking about reunion, the conversation quickly turns to "How do your adoptive parents feel about you finding your birth family?" or "Aren't you afraid to open a can of worms that could turn out badly?"

I count myself fortunate that I did not consult a lot of opinions before I began my journey to discover my roots. I do not believe it would have deterred me; however, it would have caused more unnecessary baggage than I already carry being a Baby Scoop Era Adoptee. You see, my whole life I was given the message that my birth story and family history didn't matter. As I was growing up, I was told my "adoption story"—not my "birth story." Why, you ask? Because my birth story was held under lock-and-key at the Cradle Adoption Agency and the Cook County Courts of Illinois. Even my parents had no access to it. I was a secret. I was a mystery to even myself. As I grew up, I would always be wondering about where my birth mother went and why nobody seemed to know who she was. I wondered where I came from but nobody had any answers for me.

Fears

Deciding to embark on a search is a huge decision that I did not take lightly. Some people (myself included) know their whole lives that they will search one day. Some people want to search but are too afraid. This is understandable. There is a giant psychological barrier to searching because in contemplating the search, one has to come face-to-face with fear. Fear of rejection. Fear of the unknown. Fear of failure. Fears that adoptees have already been experiencing at a heightened level, due to the trauma of being removed from the birth family. These fears and more will be unleashed when searching. Fear of upsetting adoptive family members, I find, is what prevents many adoptees from searching for decades.

Sometimes it is helpful in facing the fear to think about the worst possible scenario, and then psychologically attempt to cope with this outcome prior to actively searching. Decide in advance what it is you hope to gain by searching and decide that as long as you can meet at least a minimal goal, you are far better off than you are currently, by not knowing anything. If you fear upsetting somebody else's life, you will have to work through those fears and any assumptions you have been carrying around with you. Assumptions like, your mother wants nothing to do with you (statistically not true), that you are related to a bunch of idiots, or any other number of fears that will develop based on what you have been told by your family, society or especially yourself.

If it will be helpful to you, you can talk to your adoptive family about how you want to search and see what kind of support you receive. Some people are surprised at the level of acceptance they will get from family members. Of course, there is the risk that adoptive family members will not be understanding and in fact, could be quite upset. That is why it is especially helpful to speak with other adoptees who have taken this journey before you. I strongly recommend a competent therapist to help resolve any emotional issues that come up before, during or after locating your birth family. In my own case, I came to accept that my adoptive mother would be upset, but that I was willing and able to deal with any fallout and continue on in my search.

Who Am I? Where Did I Come From?

As I became a young adult, the questions of who I was and where I came from became more pronounced. Every time somebody asked me if I was Italian, Greek or

Spanish, I would feel this sick reminder that I didn't really know who I was. I usually would not lie; I would tell the truth. I could see the truth made people uncomfortable. Or they would think my life was this big novelty and ask lots of questions that I simply had no answers to. Most people just couldn't identify with someone who didn't know where they came from. I can't blame them. I couldn't even understand it myself.

In my early twenties, I contacted my adoption agency for my Non-Identifying Information (NII). I received it on my 25th birthday: December tenth. I read it with fascination and learned for the first time some basic facts about my birth family. There wasn't enough in there to satisfy my curiosity; however, I put the papers away and got on with life. I got married, had a son and was living the normal middle class lifestyle in Dayton, Ohio, trying not to think about who my people were. This strategy never seemed to work well for me. The truth was and has always been that I *needed* to know. However, it wasn't until my mid-to-late thirties that I realized I absolutely had a *right* to know.

You Have a Right to Know

Once you get past the fear of searching, embracing your *right* to search is another barrier that can knock an adoptee out of the game. People will tell you outright that you don't have a right to know. My adoption agency and the laws in Illinois didn't think I had a right to know when they sealed my birth certificate and refused to tell me who my mother was. My parents didn't think I had a right to know. Strangers and lovers of adoption, many times, didn't think I had a right to know because "If my mother wanted me, she would have kept me," or "Your family are the people who raised you." Many people who don't understand how it feels to be adopted think that secrets and lies are o.k. Having their own family history, they sometimes believe it is perfectly fine that I didn't have mine. Somehow that toxic thinking affected not only laws, but attitudes in society about adoptees. Somehow, because a woman gave birth and decided not to raise me, others believe it is fine that I am treated differently—like a second class citizen. Secrets and lies hurt me as a child and they continue to hurt me as an adult. When these realities about my life knocked me to the ground, I back got up and decided, "This is my birth right and I will take it back."

The Search

I can't put my finger on what specifically prompted me to begin actively searching, but I think I just finally had to answer the call in my heart after pushing it aside for so long. I was finally at my wit's end with filling out one more medical history form with "adopted" and telling one more person "I may be Italian." Enough was enough.

I began my search by filling out an adoptee record at Adoption.com. I met other adoptees in the forums of

Adoption.com and chatted with adoptees who were searching. One day I was reading something from another Illinois adoptee about our birth names being listed on our adoption papers. Years prior, my mother had given me my adoption file. I'd read through the paperwork but I hadn't really studied this treasure that resided in a storage box. I pulled out the dusty file and realized that my birth name had been there all along. I was referred to as "Baby Girl." The adoption agency had told my parents the name was a nickname so I never gave it much thought. The name was "Unger." I finally had a name, and a heritage: German.

After that small but significant success, I decided to sign up for the Illinois Adoption Registry—Medical Information Exchange (IARMIE). This would enable my birth mother to find me if she too had signed up. Unfortunately, she had neither signed up for that registry or the registry at my adoption agency and in fact, had no contact with the agency since my relinquishment. This was interpreted by one of my adoptive family members as an indication that she didn't want to be found. At the time, I wasn't sure what to think, but I didn't want to believe my birth mother did not want to know me, so I pressed on.

I began researching at the library and requesting information on Unger families in the Evanston, Illinois area. I sent letters, emails and my husband spoke with people on the phone. After plugging away at this for a while, we realized the Ungers could have literally lived anywhere in the U.S. and decided finding them was too daunting a task, four decades later with likely name changes.

Action Steps to Take

If you have not already done so, request your Non-Identifying Information from the adoption agency or Court where you were adopted. This will give you general information about your birth parents, such as eye color, hair color, height, family situation, ethnicity and birth order. Sometimes you will get more; sometimes less, depending on how well the information gatherer kept the record. This NII is helpful in your search, although many times it is incorrect. Don't put too much hope into the information or take the NII to heart.

Either ask your parents for your adoption file or attempt to get any adoption records you can from the Court. Read your adoption papers thoroughly and you will see who your adoption attorney was if you have no agency. Adoption attorneys are rarely helpful, but it might give you a lead in researching legal notices from the time around your birth. Many times these were published in legal journals.

Other important documents to gather when searching, if you can get your hands on them, are your original birth certificate (not your amended one), and hospital records from your birth (believe it or not, some hospitals still have these on microfiche). If you can access your adoption paperwork, it might list your birth name like mine did. Even though my birth name did not lead me to my birth family, had I used a private investigator or search angel, he/she may have been able to crack my case with only my birth mother's name. If you live in a state where there is a birth index (like in my state of Ohio), you can find a search angel to access the index or go to the Vital Statistics and look through the birth index. If you live in a state that allows adoptees to have access to their original birth certificates, order it immediately.

If you were adopted through an agency, inquire whether they offer post-adoption services. I eventually paid my agency $500.00 to find my birth mother. They had access to my file when I did not, so they were my best hope. Fortunately, my birth mother had an uncommon married name and she was found within one week. If you are not adopted through an agency or were adopted through an agency that does not offer post-adoption services, check to see if your state offers a confidential intermediary service. I have heard good and bad about CIs, so it is the luck-of-the-draw on who is assigned to your case. That person will have direct contact with your birth family member and you will not. You will have a passive role and if your birth family does not want contact, then you will get no closer to any information. It's a risk but if you have no luck using other methods, I would personally try it.

Many people use search angels or private investigators in order to keep some control in their own hands, using records that they do have and hope to find more information through news article databases (like Lexis/Nexis) or genealogical websites (like Ancestry), family stories or rumors, the Non-ID and a little bit of luck. If you have a really good search angel, you might find a family member faster than you can imagine. It happened to my friend who was searching for her birth daughter. A search angel found her in one day.

Facebook has a plethora of connections, groups and ways to search. There are many, many recent success stories of adoptees who took a picture of themselves holding a sign with their known birth information, asking friends and family to forward the picture and once the right person sees that picture, a reunion is the result. If you are not on Facebook and are searching, do not miss the opportunity to connect with other adoptees, search angels and the access to updates on laws allowing the release of adopted people's birth certificates.

DNA is the latest trend in finding out family information. I have taken both Family Tree DNA and 23 and Me DNA tests. I was finally able to learn my ethnic background at the age of 47. I like to say, "DNA doesn't lie," and many adoptees find that their birth mothers have lied about who their fathers are. Paternity tests can rule out fathers, but autosomal DNA tests like the ones mentioned above can link you to your mother or father's family (assuming any cousins are in the database). It was recommended to me to do both FTDNA and 23andMe DNA tests, as there are different people in the different databases. These databases are growing every day and you will continue to be notified of new matches as they become available.

Reunion Conclusion

I have been searching for several decades now and I'm always surprised at what new information I am able to find about my family. I have a wonderful editor who has researched my family tree on Ancestry.com. Every day he is sending me emails about something else he has found, including that I am related to a famous writer and painter. I treasure this information all the more, since I was never allowed to have it growing up. I still am trying to unravel secrets and lies at the age of 47. I can think of far better ways to spend my money and energy and the novelty of my life never seems to wear off for friends and acquaintances. But this is my life and I have embraced it with all its craziness. Seeing the faces of my mother, sister, brother, cousin and many other distant relatives has finally brought me the peace in my life that was missing for so long.

Seeing documented proof that there were musicians, artists and writers in in my family line, has helped me to accept and embrace my own talents and feel part of a family larger than the one I could have ever imagined before I embarked on my search.

Lynn Grubb is a Baby Scoop Era adoptee who is active in adoptee rights. She is married to Mark—a kind and patient non-adoptee—and lives in a suburb of Dayton, Ohio with their nineteen-year-old son and nine-year-old daughter. Lynn is a paralegal and has volunteered as a Court Appointed Special Advocate (CASA), which ignited her passion for children's rights. Lynn blogs at No Apologies for Being Me and The Lost Daughters.

Clarity Questions

1. Lynn states that your birth story is your birth right. Do you agree? Does it matter if you are adopted or non-adopted?

2. The author's process of not only realizing that she needed to search, but of the search itself was time-consuming and expensive. Is it worth it, in your opinion?

What are your thoughts on the time and money involved? Should adoptees pay these costs, if not adoptees, than who?

Part 3

Things Don't Always Turn Out the Way We Want,

Or,

When Reunion Isn't All Flowers and Rainbows

Chapter 9

I Have My Non-Identifying Information,

So Why Do I Need to Reunite?

By Laura Dennis

What's all this hoopla about reunion? What's so important about DNA? I prefer to leave well-enough alone.

I'm adopted; the people who raised me are my mom and dad. That's enough family for me. My adoption agency provided me with all the information I need.

I get asked this a lot.

A few months ago, I might have let bygones-be-bygones and agreed with that old adage about adoptees falling into one of two categories:

> A. Adoptees who want and need to search, and,

> B. Adoptees who decidedly do not.

I've seen the latter group *say* that they are at peace with their adoptions and adamantly affirm they possess no need to search. I *might* have even kept quiet about my view that those who don't search likely have deep-rooted post-adoption issues which so inexorably intertwined with their sense of self and family, that they fear reuniting could unravel their entire lives.

But I can keep quiet no longer! Here's the truth … You believe you know the whole story? Think again, my friend. Think again.

At the time of adoption, adoptive parents often receive Non-Identifying Information (NII) either a written document or information provided orally and jotted down by adoptive parents. The NII ostensibly states *some* biological information about the adoptee's origins.

Here's the rub … There was no *oath* required of adoption agencies. There was no promise to tell the truth, the whole truth and nothing but the truth. Birth families weren't required to give accurate information, and agencies hardly did any corroborating. In some adoptions, birth parents didn't even use their real names! *That's shenanigans right there.*

Lies Agencies Tell (or) Why You Should Search

My friend, adoptee Lynn Grubb, who wrote the

previous article, "Your Story: Your Birthright," received the results from Population Finder, which uses information from the Stanford University database (the Human Genome Project) to map DNA and ethnic heritage. These services can also be used to find biological relatives. In her No Apologies for Being Me blog post, "My Ethnicity Revealed (sort of)," Lynn stated that she's Northern European, which she knew was from her mom's side, because they're in reunion. Lynn also learned she's Native American (Central American) and Middle Eastern (Jewish), which would therefore be from her father's side. *That's cool, right?*

But her NII letter stated her father was: "A citizen of Peru, thought to be Italian born." Well played, adoption agency, well played.

But really, who cares about height, weight and ethnicity, anyway?

The thing is, agencies often wrote down whatever they thought might sound good. They lied to birth moms, as well. Take Sam's* story:

Mine was a private attorney adoption. When I made a visit to his office, the attorney was surprised I had my Original Birth Certificate (OBC) in my possession and said to me, "I tried to make sure there was no way my adoptions would ever be traced."

He said that the "non-identifying" information on birth mothers [he worked with] were all the same. 5'5,

Caucasian, brown hair, blue eyes. ... [My first mother] died while searching for me, but was told she had given birth to a boy, so she died thinking she was leaving a son.

Then there's Michelle's* story. Even after reunion with her birth mother, she still doesn't know the truth.

I was lied to, and so was the agency.

I cannot completely fault the agency for this, because they only believed the false information my birth mother gave them. Although, I do believe reform is needed in this area. Not sure what the answer is, but there has to be some way of digging deeper to get correct info, birth father identification, a factual ancestral profile, etc. before a child is relinquished.

My mother wanted to keep my true father's identity a secret. She lied to the agency and the name on my OBC is also a lie. (Kind of ruins the joy for me of getting my OBC in the future when my state opens up.) All of the NII information I received about my father's age, hair and eye color, height, occupation, was a lie.

The very reason for your adoption may have been a lie.

The agency may have believed they were protecting you from painful truths.

The social worker may have been protecting (read hiding) the bad behavior of the birth family individual who paid the agency fee.

There are so many stories like these. Even the very basic question so many adoptees tell themselves, "Why would I search? She didn't want me." ... The reality is that for the many birth moms, it wasn't a matter of "want," it was a matter of "couldn't," or being told (and believing) they "shouldn't" keep their child. Of having nowhere to live, no place to go if they kept their baby.

Even if the truth is painful, it's better than living a lie.

And, Mr. Big Deal, if you rely solely on the information you were told, you may never know the truth.

* Not their real names.

Clarity Questions

1. Many adoptees have no need or desire to search. How are these adoptees different than those who feel compelled to do so?

2. If you are adopted, does your Non-Identifying Information match reality? What is your opinion of this adoption agency practice?

Chapter 10

Playing House

By JoAnne Bennett

The woman's voice on the other end of the line sounded unfamiliar. As I was right in the middle of cooking dinner for my family, I paid little attention to her words, "Hi, this is your mother."

Without any hesitation, I quickly responded, "I am sorry; you must have the wrong number."

Again, the woman insisted she was my mother, but never specifically asked for anyone by name. Politely, I ended our call. At the time, it never crossed my mind that the woman on the telephone might have been the woman who had placed me for adoption at birth. I now regret being short with the woman and not asking her for more information.

Later I shared the rather odd phone call with my

adoptive mother. Her only comment was, "She couldn't be!"

Feeling bothered by her often-predictable evasiveness, I whispered under my breath, "What in the world does *that* mean?"

While growing up, I carried a mental picture of the woman who gave me life, in my heart. It was pieced together from my adoptive mother's few selective words. "You were one too many," which she threw at me from out of nowhere like a hard ball that I was supposed to know how to catch.

I imagined my birth mother with long, swaying, dark brown hair, pushing a stroller with one hand while balancing a toddler in a football grip on her waist. Early in my childhood, I learned it was just easier to keep whatever I might be feeling to myself. When I finally found the courage to search for answers about my birth mother, my adoptive mother's vague response to that random phone call didn't cross my mind.

A year or so later, with my adoptive parents' knowledge, the timing just seemed right to begin my journey. I was hoping that the image I had of my biological mother would no longer be a faint, penciled-in sketch, but rather that I could see a portrait of her as a real human being with perfections and flaws.

I wasn't a young person who needed their permission; I was a wife and mother of three children. Up until that point, I hadn't thought about trying to find out why there had always been so much mystery behind my birth story. However, surprisingly, it wasn't my birth mother who ended up disappointing me.

Feeling like a lost child who had wandered too far away from home, I had to ask strangers to help me find the answers. I never expected so much kindness along an often-bumpy road. Sitting in front of a computer one day, scanning through old records, my hope of ever meeting the woman who gave me life was shattered. The official document not only listed my birth mother's birth date, but her date of death as well. I felt somehow deceived she had been dead since I was eight years old.

Soon after discovering the unsettling truth, I was able to locate her family. Disrupting innocent lives was never my intention; I needed to find answers about my biological mother, to achieve some kind of closure. Relatives from my birth family were irritated that my adopted mother had insinuated that I was "one too many children." Even though bringing up the past brought back the sting of our mother's choices, my birth siblings believed I deserved the real story: I was conceived from an affair that helped destroy two families. It was important to them to keep their dad in a good light, but the truth was not said out of spite to me.

Alone, I grieved. I had to find out the hard way the truth that I believed my adoptive mother already knew. For years, she dangled stingy tidbits of her version of my birth story over me as a form of manipulation and control.

If she didn't know my birth mother was deceased, what was she trying to keep from telling me? The answer is in her response to that unusual telephone call... she did know, and that was one of the few times she unwittingly breathed truth into the story of my beginnings. And still, she left me with more questions than answers.

I could spend the rest of my life wondering why there were so many secrets, but I have chosen instead to share my personal heartaches as a way of showing others how important honesty is in our relationships. My belief is that most people's intentions are not meant to deliberately cause harm. In all fairness, it would often be difficult to know how much, or what to tell regarding the tough circumstances surrounding some adoptions.

Unfortunately, as children we can't put our deepest feelings into words. What I needed from my adoptive parents was for them to tell me honestly as much as they knew about the first chapters of my life. Whether I was hesitant or not to ask questions, I did want to know the truth about my beginnings. My fear was that I would be betraying those who raised me if I acted the slightest bit curious.

My adoptive mother's continual silence weighed heavily on my heart. I never even knew the reason why she chose to adopt me with her first husband, after already having a natural-born child of their own. I interpreted the secrecy to mean that mom must have experienced some tragic loss that I didn't know about, if she couldn't even share the truth with me—her daughter. For the longest time, I tried to be the perfect child, the one she obviously couldn't have on their own. I thought I would be letting my adoptive parents down if I went searching for my first mother. But in reality, I was crushed that there couldn't have been mutual respect for my feelings.

I am often asked by adoptive parents for suggestions on ways they might discuss these "delicate matters" with their child. Speaking from the depth of my own painful experiences, I hope to encourage adoptive parents to be open and honest. I also want to be the voice for adoptive children who are unable to put their feelings into words. I don't pretend to have all the answers, but I hope I can make a difference.

I've seen cases in which adoption has been an answer for truly abandoned children when they are welcomed into the arms of eagerly awaiting parents. But I have also witnessed the profound losses—cases in which adoption has been chosen by the birth parent as a temporary Band-Aid. Placing is not the perfect long-term solution for every pregnant woman dealing with difficult set of circumstances, or for the grieving child separated from their mother.

When the new mommy and daddy promise to spend the rest of their lives loving and nurturing a precious baby, the joyous homecoming reminds me of the sweet-looking stuffed animal, Paddington Bear. In the little note attached to the bear's coat it reads, "Please look after this bear. Thank you." Perhaps special-care instructions should be included for every adopted child to be shared with the new parents:

1. Reassure us that you won't love us any less if we want to know about our beginnings.

2. Please don't tell us what you think we *want* to hear or a fairytale version of our adoption story.

3. You mustn't feel we are less loyal or grateful for you, by how little or how much we want to know about our start in this world. It's understandable that you might feel uneasy or threatened, but the love we feel for you as our mother and our father never changes.

4. Please don't underestimate our inner strength to handle the reasons we were placed for adoption.

5. Please don't feel threatened if we choose to search for our birth family.

6. Please do not share your perception on why we were placed up for adoption with relatives, friends, or siblings. Be aware that unfounded information is often be repeated and misconstrued as fact.

7. Please don't make judgments about our birth mothers. We need to know that it is okay to have deep feelings for her that are separate from the ones we have for our parents who raised us.

8. No matter how the search turns out, remember we long to hear your comforting words, "I will always be here for you."

9. We hope you understand that sometimes we need to take this journey on our own, not as a way of shutting you out, but instead, as a means of closure.

10. Please don't be of the frame of mind, "I know the truth, but I am not going to tell you." Often, keeping secrets from those we love and care about can be damaging to any relationship.

JoAnne Bennett—After being placed for adoption at birth, JoAnne's journey took too many twists and turns to count, and she has spent the last 20 years trying to piece together her missing parts. Nevertheless, JoAnne reflects on her many blessings—raising three wonderful daughters alongside her loving husband of 38 years. Her passions are writing and making a difference in young people's lives. Helping children see that they have voices that truly matter is her heartfelt desire. She believes that loving out loud is a way of positively changing the world. JoAnne's most recent credits include a story in a book titled, *One for the Road,* a publication in *Chicken Soup for the Soul: Teens Talk Middle School,* and on Adoption.Net. She blogs at Stories by JoAnne Bennett.

Clarity Questions

1. The author had no idea that a death certificate was waiting on the other side of her search. Would it have been better to have left well enough alone? Why or why not?

2. What "special care instructions" would you have like to have been given to your parents?

Chapter 11

Butterfinger Heaven!

By Samantha Franklin

Just have to share this little story ...

We were recently at a local pizzeria celebrating
with my first dad for his birthday. It is always
"bittersweet" when spending time with my first family.
Cherished times, of which I can't get enough. Yet not able
to feel *fully* a part of the family, simply because they have
a whole life of history together that is like a gaping black
hole for me.

Nevertheless, I DO cherish every minute spent with
my family—both of birth and adoption. It has really only
been in the past few years I can say this, due to the
enormous grief and confusion I walked through during
those first "waking up" years. After all, adoptees aren't
supposed to care, search, or reunite with their true selves
and/or families, are they? No, we are supposed to be

grateful and never question. It is just too dangerous.

Anyway, here we were all sitting around the table, finished with pizza, and cutting my Dad's birthday cake. Because I was running around like a crazy woman trying to contain my sensory-overloaded child, I didn't notice that it was a Butterfinger (yes, the candy bar) cake. Mind you, my son has never eaten a candy bar in his short four years of existence. He has feeding issues and won't put most foods even near his mouth. (I've convinced myself that is why I've gained so much weight—I'm eating for two. Every bite I beg him to take and he refuses, goes straight into my mouth—*stress*). Sorry, I digress.

So my son thinks that every cake is his personal sensory experiment, to use as finger paint (thanks to creative therapists), and because he couldn't quite understand why I was holding him back (with great effort), he started to have a *royal* tantrum. When his aunt finally figured out what he wanted, she gladly scraped one of the many mini-Butterfinger bars off the cake and gave it to him. And much to my surprise—he immediately stuck the thing in his mouth and started nibbling on it! Amazing!

What is even more amazing (and was the purpose of this story) is that Butterfingers are my Dad's favorite candy, and low-and-behold, it was the catalyst to convince my son to actually TRY candy for the first time! I just quietly pondered this in my heart, sitting there wondering if I should have shared how surprised I was at my Dad's preference, because Butterfingers are also MY favorite candy bar! I can't count the number of Butterfinger sundaes I've had from Sonic's new dollar menu.

All this is trivial, EXCEPT to an adoptee. It is amazing to find out these little (and yet significant) similarities with your family of birth. And believe me, this is just one of the little things. Most of the similarities are HUGE—likes, dislikes, personality traits, voice inflection and tone, non-verbal communication gestures—so much is alike. They were inside me. Part of me. Without my knowing. All the while battling low self-esteem from NOT knowing and not being able to see my reflection in anyone else. Wondering and wandering, instead of embracing who I was and where I came from. All because it would hurt too much to deal with it. It still hurts. But it also brings understanding, identity, empathy, and joy—just to see myself in them. My whole clan. Each relative reflects a little different part of myself back to me. In my son. My mother, father, aunts, uncles, cousins, brothers. Grandparents and great-grandparents. I am so blessed to be reunited with them and love them very much.

I can't emphasize enough that it wasn't until I crossed the threshold of search and reunion (just the beginning of the journey) into grieving and healing, that I could look in the mirror and feel real and learn to really love.

Samantha Franklin is a wife, mother, and reunited adoptee. She enjoys spending time with her adoptive and birth family, who all live in the same town in Oklahoma, where she also grew up. Holidays are especially interesting because of this, but so worth it. She is an activist for adoptee access to their original birth certificates and blogs at Neither Here Nor There.

Clarity Questions

1. Non-adopted and adopted alike, we want to see ourselves reflected in our genetics. There's a name for it: genetic mirroring. How important to you was this mirroring growing up? What about if you have (or don't) have children?

2. One catalyst for search and reunion is often an adoptee becoming a parent. Suddenly genetics become important, when before it was "just DNA," "just blood." What are your thoughts about this change?

Chapter 12

Tenacity for the Truth, an Inherited Trait

By Rhonda Noonan

They called me Baby Kim. DHS, Department of Health Services of Oklahoma, that is. They said it was my "alias name." How silly that seems. I was just a baby, not a criminal. A crime was being perpetuated, however. I was being assigned a new identity, and my roots hidden from me; beyond my reach for the next fifty-three years.

My mother shares the story of her first telling me of my adoption when I was two years old. "Honey," she lovingly began, "are you my special adopted little girl?" I turned my head away, shaking it adamantly in disagreement. She was surprised by my reaction. Adopted was not what I wanted to be. It meant something had gone wrong. Terribly wrong. Of course I knew all about it. I was there.

Growing up, I would look in the mirror and wonder where I came from. My grandmother had told me the "story" given the family by the "department." Even as a youngster, it seemed to me to be a lie. "Your family," she explained, "they were famous." That comment, passed on to her by a social worker, was lost to me, in the bigger story, as my grandmother stated, "We'll never know for sure."

The feelings of uniqueness and loneliness, described by so many adoptees, were well-known to me. They had much less to do with the way I looked and more to do with how I thought; how I viewed the world, and what I believed. In the midst of a loving, terrific family, I was all alone. There was a profound sadness always within immediate reach that reminded me of the grief that was mine days after my birth. I wondered how I could have been so unlovable as to be given away and forgotten.

Life goes on and time passes. I graduated college, started teaching and began my "adult" life. None of that really mattered much to me in comparison with a far more important event: I was told I had a grandfather who had loved me—a BIOLOGICAL grandfather. The idea of such a person smacked head-long into my long-held belief that no one had loved me; no one had cared or given me a second thought. What if that were true? It was a game-changer; a life saver. I had to find him.

My love affair with my grandfather began that day. I imagined a loving, wise, compassionate man, whom, I suspected, had a rather strong character to have been the ONE family member who really cared about me. Perhaps he protested the treatment of me. I hoped so. I hoped I would find him alive.

Twenty-nine years later, I look at pictures of that grandfather, Sir Winston Churchill, and see my face; the same face that wondered, looking in the mirror, who on this Earth looked like me. As a teenager, I hated my "pug" nose and the way I looked mad, even when I was just sitting expressionless. I have my father's legs, hands, and teeth, and my grandfather's arching eyebrow that communicates emphasis or warning as needed. I have a much more complete sense of self. I have my beginning and the story of my relatedness—my people—through time and history.

I have learned that there are few things in life as valuable as the truth; the sheer power of which cannot be contained. The truth cannot be hidden indefinitely. It cannot be manipulated or harnessed for deception over the long haul. It fights for freedom and justice and neither time nor space can derail its mission. Every day that passes I recognize the blessing I was afforded in finding my truth. Tenacity and persistence led the way. Genetic, I suspect... courtesy of my beloved grandfather.

The following is excerpted from my book, *The Fifth and Final Name, Memoir of an American Churchill*:

As I investigated further, I learned that some historians believe Sir Winston himself was likely illegitimate. I knew he had an American mother and a detached and distant relationship with his father. He certainly could have felt compassion for my parallel plight.

But at the same time I was reading all these things, I couldn't get my mind around the possibility that a man of such historical significance could be the man I had been searching for these thirty years. It blew my mind to contemplate the possibility that Winston Churchill could be my grandfather.

I sat and looked at photos of Randolph, and the most shocking one of all was the only close-up of his teeth; I thought, oh my gosh—there are *my* teeth. Prior to having my teeth capped and fixed, they were identical to his.

I noticed his legs, the way he stood, even the way he walked. I realized I had the same gait. Of course, internally, I wasn't convinced. I thought it must all be an amazing coincidence... and just as quickly dealt with the reality that I don't believe in coincidences.

And as if to confirm this, I found a video of Randolph's appearance on a 1956 TV show called *What's*

My Line. There is a shot of his hand in which he appears to sport a signet ring with a "C" and dark background—exactly like the ring Lillie [a psychic and decades-long confidant] described being worn by the man present as I was handed over to the state at two months old. Bingo! I searched to establish a time frame for the taping of the show. It aired in February 1956 but the recording date eluded me.

I asked myself, how on earth could Randolph Churchill be responsible for me? What would he have been doing in Oklahoma?

The references to President Truman and his wife, Bess, were equally perplexing. Not having information from my birth mother about the events immediately following my delivery, it was impossible to know how the former president might have assisted with the adoption. Clearly Truman was a friend of the Churchills, and the state of Missouri had been mentioned in readings before.

All of this seemed stranger than fiction. You just couldn't make it up.

The more carefully I studied Averell Harriman, the more I realized that his relationship with Raymond Gary had been a close one, politically. The Democrats were looking at Gary as a possible vice-presidential candidate should Harriman win the nomination. And as I researched newspaper articles I learned that Gary had traveled to New York City to meet Harriman just prior to the premier of the musical *Oklahoma*. They took publicity photos for the play.

Lillie had always talked about my grandpa being British and at "the level of a president." She knew that my grandfather and father were already deceased; that my father had a tumultuous relationship with his father, and that my mother would have been way below his social class. She said my family was steeped in history, and that my "grandfather would be in history books." She had talked about race horses and alcoholism, and...

My mind was swimming. I contemplated my common sense... or lack thereof. How could this be?

It wasn't long after this that I learned my mom wanted to call and talk to my birth mother. She asked if I was okay with it. I thought it would be interesting to hear what Pat might say, but doubted sincerely that she would talk to Mom at all. In fact the request never even reached her. I dialed the phone for Mom, and Zippy answered. I told her my mom wanted to talk to Pat. Zippy explained there was "no way," and that was the end of that.

Mom was disappointed, saying she only wanted to thank Pat for "giving me such a wonderful child." I, on the other hand, was relieved that I didn't have to worry about Mom's feelings being hurt. Knowing where Pat stood, it didn't seem a good idea for them to speak. What a strange collision of maternal characters that might have been: one woman who had been swimming in kids and had abdicated her role as mother; another who had been childless, and climbed mountains to secure her role as mother.

We hung up the phone and slid back into our daily routines.

Weeks turned into months, and one day Zippy said, "Let's have you come down for lunch—with Mother. I'll ask Lenore and Glenda to join us."

So we planned a date for the four of us and Pat. I drove to Zippy's, walked in, and sat down at the table. There we were for the first time since my "blackmail" attempt.

During the entire two hours we were there, Pat Nail spoke no more than twice. She sat at one end of the table, and I sat to one side. Every time I would look at my sisters, in my peripheral vision I could see her watching me. But not one single time did she look me in the eye when I looked at her. Can you imagine?

I said one thing to her during the entire meeting, and she responded with a single sentence. And at another point she spoke another sentence—she told Zippy to turn the fan off because she didn't want it blowing on her food when we ate. It was fascinating in that I have never, in my life, been comfortable eating food under a blowing ceiling fan. I have been known by friends to get up and turn off a fan when food was served.

The lunch was delicious, but the event was uncomfortable. When we were leaving, Pat clearly avoided making any move in my direction as I was hugging my sisters. She might have succeeded if not for

Zippy saying, "Mom get over here, and give her a hug."

Pat obeyed. I had zero desire to hug someone who clearly did not want to hug me, but I decided to go with the flow, then leave as fast as possible without making anyone feel uncomfortable or awkward. She hugged me and walked away.

It had become more than clear at this point that Pat was never going to be cool with me. Zippy had told me she thought Pat might actually try to normalize things between us. I took that to mean that she would build a façade of social responsibility and acceptability, and even if not genuine, keep up some appearances. But after that day, I knew it would never happen. She told Zippy, "Now, maybe she will go away." I never saw Pat again.

I felt compassion for my birth mother and was acutely aware of the fact that she had never wanted to deal with me; that I had pushed this nasty secret on her. But I never understood her position, and she never shed any light on it. How could a mother not want to see her child? My sisters had embraced me; I was thankful for that. Surely that had been reassuring to Pat. Unfortunately, she wasn't letting anyone in on what had actually happened to her all those years ago.

I believed she had been threatened and treated badly; probably she was told very clearly what she was to do with me. It might well have been a horrifying time for her. Something made her see me as a problem all those years later. Pat had told DHS that she felt no affection for my father; that she had not known him. My sisters had shared with me that, despite the fact that it was two years after my birth that Pat dated Robert Mosier, she had cared a great deal for him. If he had been my father, she would not have spoken so negatively about him. None of it made any sense!

Clearly it had not been an easy situation for her. She seemed to be harboring real anger about the circumstances surrounding my birth; I simply could not comprehend why that anger was directed towards *me*. Was the whole Robert Schultz charade forced on her? Perhaps the clairvoyant I had consulted was correct. Maybe she was threatened in ways I cannot imagine. Perhaps she believed silence was necessary to protect her family from harm. I did not appreciate her silence but I tried to understand it.

My birth mother would dislike me to her grave, and there would never be a blasted thing I could do about any of it. As I have always believed that things happen the way they are supposed to, I tried to simply accept what was.

I was talking to Zippy one day, and she told me that Lenore had read an article in the *Oklahoman* which mentioned something about Lloyd Rader having kept daily logs and records which were maintained at the University of Central Oklahoma. Zippy thought it would be wise to check there for anything that might remotely relate to my adoption. So I investigated.

I contacted a woman at UCO who said some of the records were publicly available and some weren't, and I would just have to show up and discuss all that in person. So, I went down there and was given piles and boxes of stuff. I was buried in materials—thousands of pages. I very quickly realized there was vastly more there than I could get through in a millennium. Only a small amount of the data was cataloged chronologically. I looked for 1955 and 1956, but there was nothing specific about adoptions—*anyone's* adoption.

It had been another good idea, and I'm glad I made the effort, but it yielded nothing. I had to find someone else directly related to my history.

Of course, always in the back of my mind was Randolph Churchill and any possibility that he was in Oklahoma City.

Rhonda Noonan earned an Associate's degree from Northern Oklahoma College, and Bachelors and Masters degrees from Northeastern State University, Tahlequah, Oklahoma. Her career in mental health spans almost thirty years and includes stints as the Director of Clinical Services at five inpatient psychiatric facilities in Oklahoma and Colorado. She has spent much of her career working with adoptees and their families. Find *The*

Fifth and Final Name, Memoir of an American Churchill on Amazon.

Clarity Questions

1. It took resilience, gumption and decades of persistence for the author to uncover the truth of her origins. Many non-adoptees genuinely wonder why adoptees feel such a deep need to search. At so many points, it would have been easier simply to give up. Should Rhonda have just let sleeping dogs lie? Should she have stopped searching and been satisfied with her life in her loving adoptive family?

2. Adoptees dreaming of having been relinquished by a famous first mother or father—that's classic 'ghost kingdom' fantasizing, in which adoptees dream of what their life might have been like had they not been adopted. In this case, Rhonda was adopted out of the Churchill family, the FBI was involved, her name was changed five times—on five different legal documents—just to keep the truth buried as deeply as possible. It turns out, it was all real. She was/is from a famous family. What are your thoughts on the ghost kingdom as they relate to secrets and lies?

Chapter 13

Reunion Once Removed

By Corie Skolnick

My father was just seventeen years old when the Japanese bombed Pearl Harbor in December of 1941, and like a lot of American boys, he was swept up in patriotic fervor. He tried to enlist in the U.S. Navy but was told that he had to return to the recruitment office with a birth certificate and a parent to give permission. The family legend held that my grandmother resisted on both counts. For a while she swore up and down that she had lost my father's birth certificate and anyway she did not want to sign papers giving him permission to enlist so young. Eventually (so the story went) he wore her down. My mother always said that Grandma only relented because my father promised to send home his service pay. In any event, finally Grandma produced a birth certificate. The only problem was, my father's name was not on it.

How strictly accurate this account is might be questionable. What was never questioned was my mother's antipathy toward my father's mother. There was never any doubt that my mother considered my grandmother and her scandalous behavior in the most negative terms. She judged her harshly and spared her little sympathy even though Grandma had been just sixteen years old when she had my dad. That fact alone was enough in my mom's judgment to convict my grandmother of very serious moral deficiencies. I'm pretty sure that Grandma's negative character traits were exaggerated by my mother while anything that might have been seen as good was negated. My mother was a reflection of society as a whole at that time. Getting pregnant outside of marriage was a serious offense and there were words for girls like that. My mom never let my dad forget his illegitimate origins.

Regardless of either accuracy or my mom's negative judgment of Grandma's moral character, that is nevertheless how my father, at the tender age of seventeen, found out that he was the "bastard" son of a man he'd never heard of, and that another man he'd known as his father (and indeed his namesake) was no relation to him at all, except to be the biological father of his younger siblings and his mother's then ex-husband. At just seventeen years of age then, my dad joined the Navy using his new "real" name and off he went to war. (How very young he was and indeed how very "small" he was at age seventeen came home to me once when I found his Navy "blues" packed away in our basement. I tried them on, thinking at the time that I could use his uniform for a Halloween costume or some such thing. I remember clearly calculating how slender my father had been once upon a time when at age fourteen weighing 112 pounds myself at just over five foot four, I could not button his pants!) When my dad enlisted as a U.S. sailor, he was just a skinny kid.

You might wonder about my use of the word "bastard" in relation to my father. In the online dictionary there are four definitions for the word bastard used as a noun. Three of them are, in order, "offensive terms" for "somebody regarded as obnoxious and disagreeable," for "somebody born to unmarried parents," and for "something that is extremely difficult, trying or unpleasant." By virtue of the circumstances of his birth, my dad was definitely the middle definition. Anyone who knew him could tell you that at any given time he was perfectly capable of qualifying for the other two definitions as well. The fourth definition, "something that is inferior, debased, or of questionable or mixed origin (sometimes considered offensive)," was, I believe, my dad's "felt sense" about who he was in the world for most of his life. I believe that much of what seemed confusing, even contradictory; about my father was in part, compensation for those feelings. I think that society's pejorative attribution—bastard—left its mark on my father's identity, and on his life, and consequently on ours, too.

In historical context, to be a bastard in the America of the nineteen forties and fifties was a burden that is almost unimaginable in modern society. To be sure, the shame of revealed sexuality fell on girls and women disproportionately, but the shame and social stigma of illegitimacy were also borne by the children who were conceived outside of marriage. Lives and careers were ruined and fortunes were lost when scandal in the form of unwanted and illegitimate pregnancy affected a family. Even so, I don't believe that my dad's "issues" were so much related to his illegitimacy as they were about what he believed to be his abandonment by his father. I have come to believe that it was the loss of his father, this "orphan-ness" that made him feel inferior and "debased."

"What issues?"—you might well ask.

Can we stipulate here that a written, undocumented postmortem on the personality of one's father is almost always a hazardous endeavor, perhaps especially so for a psychotherapist, and its undertaking is fraught with anxiety. So, again, it would be within reason for you to ask—"Why do it?"

To write honestly about my dad and his reunion story requires that I acknowledge my inheritance. His issues are my issues, too. His feelings of inferiority and his sense of himself as inadequate are mine, too. His fear of rejection and his coping strategy of failure to adequately and securely attach are known to me as my own. If I examine my father's life, if I scrutinize and study it, I have to hope that I might find wisdom, insight, and even change. Change before it's too late for me, as it was for my dad.

Ironically, in a very real way, I spent most of my life in a search for my father. Not in a physical sense. Physically he was present. If he wasn't at home, we knew where he was, and really, he very rarely went anywhere except to work. But when he was home, you never knew exactly "who" was there. As a therapist, burdened by theory, I've often thought that my father was slightly dissociative. Such a theory explains a lot about the complexity of my father's personality. It explains why you never knew who you would encounter. He could be intensely compassionate on one occasion and unbelievably, even cruelly callous on another. He was prone to temper tantrums and provoked to physically threaten even violence against his children. Other times he seemed remote to the point of oblivion. He read voraciously yet never once had what you might consider even a mildly intellectual discussion with any of us. Reading, for my father, was an escape, and where it was he escaped to nobody else was welcome. You might expect, and it was the case, that my mother resented his reading and only one of his five children can read for pleasure with utter abandon. Myself, I feel to this day, tremendously almost painfully guilty whenever I am "not doing anything" which means, in my mother's judgment, I am reading. My father could be congenial and unimaginably generous, with his time and his resources, even money, and then in a heartbeat he could be as stingy as Scrooge and as uncooperative and negative and paranoid as any crazed Libertarian survivalist.

I have come to believe that it was not his actions, egregious as some were, that made life as his child so difficult. Truly, what made life in our house so unalterably confusing was the lack of predictability. We literally never knew what, or more precisely who to expect. This insane unpredictability drove us to our mother for almost everything and created an imbalance in the authority structure that undoubtedly gave birth to some of those aforementioned "issues" that each of us has grappled with in different ways as adults. It made my father unapproachable and, in a very real way, "lost" to us. He simply could not be trusted to take you seriously or to respond thoughtfully rather than make fun of your concerns or react irrationally. Even much later in life, when I made sincere attempts to inquire about his own thoughts and feelings, and in fact when I tried to engage him in some open and honest exchange of both, he rebuffed my invitations and rebuked me meanly as a "sick-chologist." When he died last year I felt that I had never really known him. This feeling seems to me a perfect metaphor for his own relationship with his father.

It may have been somewhat uncharacteristic of my father to have done so, but he did search for and find his birth father some ten years after finding out about him. My grandmother had just enough information about my grandfather's extended family to make it possible, even relatively easy, for them to reunite, and they did, albeit only one time. By then my father was a father-of-three himself, and maybe that is why, when they met at a coffee shop in Minnesota, several hundred miles north of where we lived in Chicago, my dad who was around twenty-seven at the time, declined his own father's invitation to meet his two teenaged brothers. My mother was at that meeting. She said that their incredible physical resemblance made any question about paternity moot. My grandfather acknowledged that he had always kind of wondered about the possibility that my grandmother had had a child. He did not question that my father was his first born son, but he claimed that she was the one who disappeared without a trace. By my mother's account he was willing to "come clean" to his wife and children. My father saw no good reason for it. He always said that he didn't want to "upset the old man's applecart." To my knowledge there was only minimal correspondence between them after that solitary meeting and my grandfather died without telling my dad's two half-brothers that my father even existed. That is not the end of my father's reunion story however. The conclusion of that story, like my dad himself, is a mixed emotional bag.

Some of it sad, some a little tragic even, and some, sweetly touching. Like many reunion stories, his is bittersweet.

It was my youngest brother, many years later, who searched for and found my dad's half-brothers, and then facilitated their "reunion." I recently asked him what made him reach out to them just when he did. He speculated that it was in part because he had recently married and was leaving Illinois to move across country. Perhaps, he said, he felt some compulsion to find them before they were lost to us. My younger brother exhibits a sentimentality that my father has shown only in the briefest of glimpses.

Even without the Internet, it had proved easy to locate them and just before moving, my brother made a phone call to the oldest "uncle." It was awkward, he said, but not awful. Given the circumstances, the man was, if not enthused, at least he did not realize my brother's worst fears and just hang up. It took him nearly ten years however to share the news of my father's existence with his younger brother. By then, Mike (my brother) had met with "Uncle" Fred several times in Las Vegas where he then lived. He started to pressure Fred to tell his younger brother about my dad, and when Fred balked, Mike advised him that if he didn't do it, Mike would do it himself. Under pressure, Fred called "Uncle" Don and arranged a meeting. We were told later that Don was quite upset that Fred had unilaterally decided to keep my father's existence a secret from him. He immediately contacted my father and arranged to meet. This hastened a reunion of all three brothers.

What I know of the ensuing relationship among these three adult men, I know only from secondhand accounts and from direct observation on only two occasions when I was in their mutual presence. Even so I would testify under oath to the witness of a miraculous change in my father's demeanor when he was with "his brothers" that I never saw under any other circumstances. The change was remarkable, but sadly, short lived. My father was congenial and warm towards them. The constant contempt that seemed always lurking just below the surface was never exhibited in their presence. My father seemed quite simply relaxed and consistently just plain "nice," and I'm a little ashamed to say that I felt a twinge of jealousy that these two strangers seemed to get the best moments of my father. I know that they met a few more times in the final decade of my father's life and it's entirely possible that his affect deteriorated, but I hope not. I hope that my father was given something by those relationships that none of us could provide.

Dementia set in several years prior to his death and the most objectionable features of his personality only intensified with its progression. He became only more of who he had always been and so even more remote and unavailable. He became a caricature of hostility and sometimes grief. It was difficult, if not impossible to love him.

I never thought of my father as an "orphan" even though the reality of his childhood included periodic abandonment and severe neglect by his mother and he grew up never knowing his father at all. Although I was certainly aware of the details of this history, and I instinctively knew that he was a damaged man, I was, like all of us, in denial of the emotional and psychological impact that his history had on his development (and on his children). Ours was not a psychologically sophisticated household. We did not have the knowledge nor the education to identify my father's behavior accurately. We did not have the language to describe it. Even as an adult and a practicing therapist, it was years before I could acknowledge the likely cause of my father's sometimes bizarre behavior and call it what it was. Our family was not unlike families with adopted children that for years, even decades, simply deny the reality of the child's loss and grief in spite of a lot of acting out. It could never be acknowledged in the context of my father's violence that his history included abandonment and terror and grief. Psychological treatment was absolutely out of the question. It is no wonder that my chosen profession was a threat to his carefully constructed denial system. It is no wonder that he resisted any empathy or intimacy. As understandable as this is, it still feels to me a great tragedy that he could not be known by his children and neither could he summon the will to really know them. Yet, somehow, I believe that he was able to manage this at least partially with his brothers. For those few moments of real connection between them, I am very grateful.

The realization of exactly how profoundly my father was affected by his reunion with his brothers came to me only recently and from an interesting source. I'm a teacher and a therapist. I believe that we teach that which we need to learn. I also believe that our deepest, most important and most profound learning happens, not from instruction and lecture, but often at an unconscious level, and even more often through art.

In the fall of 2000, I unwittingly got on board The Adoption Train. I had been asked to teach a course at California State University, Northridge called, The Psychological Aspects of Parenthood. It was a course that I had taught some ten years earlier when I was newly licensed as a marriage and family therapist. The first time around, I completely neglected the topic of adoption. It simply was not mentioned once. The subject of adoption was not addressed in the chosen textbook and neither was it included in the university's suggested curriculum for the course. After a decade of private practice I learned not only how prevalent adoption was in the general population, I came to feel that my complete neglect of the topic (in a course on parenthood, no less!) was beyond simple oversight. I also wondered that not a single student complained or suggested that the subject should be included. Statistically it is not possible that not one student from that class was "touched by adoption." Yet, they hadn't "outed" themselves. Why? I could ask the question by then, but I had to teach the course again to get the answer.

I needed help with the subject so I invited a panel of speakers, volunteers from a support group called Concerned United Birthparents to address the class at CSUN. Four women, two who identified themselves as "birth mothers" and two who identified as "adoptees" showed up. They talked for almost three hours without a break and that was the beginning of my education regarding adoption. I invited them back every semester for the next five years. Along the way I started writing a novel that was influenced by the stories told in that class. *Orfan, a novel* was meant to be a fable about the fallacy of the rescue narrative in adoption, especially in transracial adoption. The book was my ticket to board the adoption train, but I always felt that because I was not a member of the adoption triad, my bona fides to write on the subject were never enough. My voice, even though the story is fiction, was suspect. Even as a mental health professional, I felt insecure among triad members who are arguably and maybe legitimately suspicious of "outsiders." Because of my book and my counseling cred, I often got invited to adoption-related events. It was one such event that finally opened my eyes to how critical my father's reunion with his brothers must have been.

Brian Stanton is an adoptee and a gifted writer and

actor. His one-man play, *BLANK* chronicles his real-life search and reunion, and I was invited by friends to see it in Los Angeles. Like many searches, Brian's originated with a search for his birth mother. *BLANK* is a magnificent piece of theatre. Like most of the others in that audience, I was moved to tears and laughed out loud. Near the conclusion of the show, I was completely derailed when Brian turned his attention as a searching adoptee to his birth father. Perhaps it was because my own father was much on my mind at the time. We had moved him into assisted living near my brother in Las Vegas. His mental function was deteriorating rapidly. He was decompensating right before our eyes. Perhaps it was how unprepared I was for Brian's brilliant piece of theatre. How unsuspecting I was that his dramatic turn could represent so accurately so much of my father's loss and need. One minute I was an admiring audience member and the next I was weeping and in shock. I felt that I had been sucker-punched. I left the theatre in a daze. I had to see the show a second time to be fully present for the end. The second time I was prepared, but my reaction was no less emotional. When I saw Brian Stanton writhing in agony, not knowing his father and not knowing as a young man if he would even want to know him … he was my dad in that moment. It was the most profound empathic experience I've ever had. I felt that for the first time I really knew the depth of my father's loss. I felt how extraordinary that loss must have been for him as a boy of seventeen.

The tragic part of this reunion story is not dissimilar to other reunion stories I have heard. Everybody didn't live happily ever after. My father never really got to know his father, but he did get to reunite with his brothers. And, by the time I felt I really knew my father, it was too late. I could not tell him all I had learned about him from watching Brian's play. I had waited too long to learn and his mind was gone and soon after he died. So what are my conclusions?

Coincidently I received an email from a woman who was reading my book. She told me a story ... an adoption story with a potential for reunion. Her mother had confided on her deathbed that she had relinquished a child in her teens. The woman wanted to know if she should search for her lost sibling in spite of resistance from her brother and his family who advised her not to "upset the applecart." She asked my advice. I told her the story about my Dad.

Corie Skolnick is the author of *Orfan, a novel.* She is a licensed California Marriage and Family Therapist and has been an adjunct faculty member in the Psychology Departments of both California State University, Northridge (CSUN) and Moorpark College.

The Comparative Literature Program at San Diego State University selected Corie and *Orfan* for the prestigious Hugh C. Hyde Living Writers Series in the Spring of 2012, and *Orfan* was nominated for the 2012-2013 Freshman Common Reading Selection at Cal State University, Northridge. Her second novel, *America's Most Eligible* will be published by MVP/MVR in 2014.

Clarity Questions

1. The author is not adopted, and yet the perceived stigma of illegitimacy follows from her father and affects Corie and her relationship with him. She says, "To write honestly about my dad and his reunion story requires that I acknowledge my inheritance. His issues are my issues, too." Sometimes we think of adoption as a one-time event: the papers are signed, and that's it. But here we see even in a step-parent, unofficial adoption situation, issues remain. Through generations. How can this cycle be broken?

2. Was yours a "psychologically sophisticated household" growing up? What about today?

3. What are your views on 'upsetting the applecart'?

Chapter 14

Finding Earl

By Trace DeMeyer

I was born on Sept. 9, 1956 and officially adopted July 3, 1958. I'd been placed in an orphanage then two foster homes. I was determined to find out what happened and why. In 1994, I met my natural father Earl and we had our reunion. Some of this story is taken from my memoir One Small Sacrifice.

I had three years to summon more courage. I had no choice but to write Helen, my birthmother, one last time in September 1994. I mailed her a birthday card. In a few short sentences, I demanded she send me the name of my father, or I'd go on a talk show or hire a lawyer. I gave her 30 days.

My patience had grown thin. I had searched for my

birthmother since 1979. A judge in Wisconsin let me read my adoption file and from that I had her name. Helen refused to meet me when I finally found her in 1991. My first letter to Helen was a few pages long and I explained how I'd hoped to meet her, and I'd enclosed three photos of me at different ages. She returned everything and wrote, **do not** contact me again. I then tried contacting others in her family in Wisconsin and finally figured out only Helen could tell me who my father was. Writing her in 1994 was my last resort, my only hope for reunion.

This time it took two weeks for my birthmother to write me back:

"Your father and I never kept in touch—however I hope you can get the information you need. His name was Earl Bland of Pana, Illinois and any other facts have left my memory. I don't know if he is even alive anymore."

This time, she signed her name: Helen Becker. (The envelope had her address label which surprised me, but I respected her wish that I never contact her again.)

That same day I called the police department and asked them to deliver a message to Earl because his phone number was unlisted.

That afternoon I got a call from William, the oldest of Earl's five kids he'd raised. William was calling from my father's phone.

My birthfather wanted to talk to me. This was it, my moment of truth. My heart was racing.

Earl and I talked a long time the first time. I had

questions. I asked if he had lived with a woman in Chicago whose name was Helen Thrall. *Yes.* I asked if he knew he had got her pregnant. *Not exactly.* I asked, "Are we American Indian?" Earl laughed, *Yes, of course.* Then we both laughed. We are also Irish, which explains our blue eyes. (Knowing this side of my ancestry was like a ton of mystery lifted. I had thought about this incessantly since I was 12.)

My father told me about our family and especially his mother's mother, Granny. Mary Francis Morris-Harlow was a full-blood Indian who had 13 kids. Mary was tiny at five feet, very petite, with hair as long as she was tall. She was a midwife. I saw her in my mind as he talked. She had even prayed with a stone pipe. (One of my cousins keeps it now.)

As promised, that same day I wrote Earl a letter explaining what I knew, when I was born and details from my adoption file. Our next call, Earl asked how soon I could get there and he agreed to have a very expensive DNA test (which my first husband Dave helped me pay for). I flew to Illinois in early November 1994. There I met my sister, four brothers, and aunts, uncles, nieces and nephews.

I had not read about reunions and how difficult they can be. I had no point of reference. I had not heard any stories from friends who were adopted and reunited with their natural parent. I was flying solo and going to Illinois alone. I just didn't know what I was getting myself into…

William and his girlfriend Brenda met me in St. Louis at the Missouri airport. I was more nervous than excited. Meeting all these new people, even if they are family, was not going to be easy for me. My brother and Brenda tried explaining everything to prepare me for meeting Earl. They said they tried to imagine how I felt. I held in too much anxiety for words so they covered a lot of information on the two-hour drive.

I wanted to believe my adoption was a mistake and something horrible had gone wrong. This reunion would solve that mystery, I'd hoped.

There was family waiting when our car pulled up. It was planned the first night I'd stay with Earl and his third wife Sheryl in their mobile home in Pana. Earl's alcoholism and emphysema had nearly ruined his health by then. He was ill but hanging on.

Walking in, even before I could sit down, Earl mumbled I did resemble my mother, shaking his head; and he made some wisecrack about "big ass." (I was too weak, too shocked to react. Alcohol allows people to say things without considering the person hearing it. I knew this from my childhood. I was speechless.)

At his kitchen table, Earl talked about his kids, other family and his life. He mentioned a son he never met, who may be a lawyer down in New Orleans. He just wasn't sure.

That first day, Dad didn't talk about Helen, my mother, his ex-girlfriend from Wisconsin. I wanted details. Maybe he didn't because his newer wife Sheryl was sitting there. She was developmentally disabled, with the mind of a 13-year-old.

When I saw a cockroach in the bathroom and in the kitchen that day, I wanted out. It would be a sleepless night. My heart would not stop racing. I felt afraid, like I did as a child.

The next morning when Earl cracked open a beer at 7 a.m., I couldn't believe my eyes! I felt a familiar pang in my gut, but again I was too fragile to say anything. I wondered to myself, "Wouldn't beer ruin our DNA test?"

Thank God William called within minutes and told me he had already cleared it with the lab that beer wouldn't affect our DNA test in Springfield, Illinois that morning. William must have known this would happen. He came over, took us to breakfast and drove us to the lab. The lab technician took Polaroid photos of me and Earl and drew our blood.

Back at his kitchen table, my father, breathing oxygen through a nose tube, hacking phlegm into a coffee can, finally told me his version of the Helen-Earl story. I believed him. (It was different than my adoption file which had Helen's version.) He said he loved me. I believed him. This scared me a little. I was accepting his words, but he was clearly intoxicated. My brain was working overtime yet my heart was reacting with happiness.

Every discussion was about Earl and his kids, so I

listened. My father never once asked how it was for me growing up. They were trying very hard to catch me up on a lifetime I missed. I couldn't possibly explain my life in just one sitting, so I let everyone else tell me about their life for an entire week. I was full of apprehension. I wanted them to like me.

I was very self-conscious, having fought a losing battle with my weight since 1984. I couldn't blame it on my pending divorce or that I had quit smoking in 1983. I had never weighed this much in my entire life. I was a size 16. My thyroid was burned out from a lifetime of stress, and I had been feeding my pain by stuffing my body. My Illinois family was thin. I stood out as this heavy person, taller than my father.

Here I was, having my reunion and I wanted to feel something other than revulsion at myself. I wanted to feel better than I did. I'd dreamed a new beginning, a new family, and a new life would happen if I found them, that it would change "me" immediately, like magic.

I could tell this was too much to process all at once. I'd walked into a potentially toxic situation, too much for me to handle. Earl, an alcoholic, was dying. This trip was about him, not me.

Butch and Brenda took me to their house my second night. My brother Danny and his wife Kathy had me over for dinner. I met my brother Terry and his wife Sue that weekend. I got a chance to meet my youngest brother Michael, 18 and just graduating from high school. He lived in Alabama with his mother's relatives. He'd left Illinois when his mother Carolyn divorced Earl. Mike didn't say anything to me. I was thinking: *I'm almost 40. I'm old enough to be his mother!*

My brothers looked more Indian than me. All have dark hair and dark eyes. My sister Teresa had brown eyes too. (I really look like Danny, according to my husband Herb who has met them.) When Earl was young he had black hair and blue eyes. My mother Helen had brown hair and blue eyes.

It was hard to miss that Earl's family was damaged by his alcohol abuse, much like my adopted father Sev hurt ours with his addiction. I asked my sister if she had been sexually molested. Earl had not abused her like Sev had abused me.

Teresa took me to visit one of Earl's sisters, my aunt Frankie, and for the first time in my life, I really did look like someone. Frankie had an oval black-and-white photo of my grandmother Lona Dell Harlow. She and I have the exact same eyebrows and brow line. I couldn't stop looking at her photo.

I knew that moment, seeing Lona, I knew for sure I'd found my family. Teresa said she knew before the DNA results, too. I have their nose and ears.

(I look nothing like my mother Helen. In 1993, I secretly met her mother/my grandmother in Wisconsin, and she showed me my mother's photo.)

A month later, the mail man delivered the lab report

that said it was a 99.9 percent match. Earl was my father. In the next days and months, my dad phoned me in Oregon. I'd moved to Rockaway on the coast for a year; I was separated from Dave and about to be divorced.

I was only able to meet Earl that one time. I knew he was very sick and I was getting regular updates on his health; I heard the day he was hospitalized. By 1996 I was working as an editor at a busy newspaper in Wisconsin and I couldn't leave my job and go to Illinois.

On September 19, 1996, at 8 p.m., Earl died. I attended his funeral in Pana. I am listed as Earl's daughter in his obituary.

Since that first reunion, I grew very close to Teresa. My husband Herb and I spent one Thanksgiving with her family in 2005 and I attended her oldest daughter's wedding. I drove back to Illinois and stayed with her in 2010. In 2012, Teresa died from Lou Gehrig's disease. I'd known her 18 years. I attended her funeral in Illinois and stayed with her husband Denny and visited with my brothers and close cousins, The Harlow Girls, as I call them. Several nieces and nephews introduced me to their kids. Funerals become sad family reunions.

One of my Harlow cousins called recently and was filling me in on how our grandparents died and their various medical conditions. She knew I needed this. She said I was the only baby "lost" in our entire family. If our grandparents had known, if Earl had known, I never would have been adopted. Her words heal me every time we talk or email on Facebook.

I feel my family's love and acceptance every phone call, every time we reunite. They really want me in their lives.

Writing History

I'm 12 and my adoptive parents took me and my brother to the famous Lumberjack Festival in Hayward, Wisconsin. Then I heard the drum. The Lac Courte Oreilles Ojibwe powwow was happening on the same grounds. The sound of the drum, the men singing filled me, like my heart opened up and the sky fell in. I could not tell anyone what I was feeling that day but it made me feel good, proud, and different. I knew I was an Indian girl, just like the other girls I saw there, but no one could tell me anything since I was adopted.

Back then life was about mystery. I knew little-to-nothing about being adopted or Indian, just that I was.

Tribes in North America call adoptees Lost Birds, Lost Children, Lost Ones and Split Feathers. Adoption messes with the brain's natural order so adoptees do split and get two experiences. One could argue which experience is best.

Adoption affecting one race of people—*American Indians*—had a specific purpose—the break-up of Indian families, to disrupt tribal culture across North America. Their idea was to assimilate us, tame us.

What is known about the Indian Adoption Projects

and the aftermath, it's pretty much been secret, but I had to know more.

Someone blogged in 2008: "Anyone who questions the Adoption Game gets thrown in jail or called crazy." Call me crazy then. Ground Zero for me was 2004, when I decided to write about it. I decided to do research on adoption in Indian Country, the Indian Child Welfare Act and finally write about my journey and reunion. My memoir came out in 2010 and my anthology, *Two Worlds: Lost Children of the Indian Adoption Projects*, was published in 2012.

Adoption "secrecy" makes my work nearly impossible. As a journalist I soon discovered nothing about adoption is simple or open; not after 1,000 drafts of my memoir, not after reading my file at age 22 back in 1979.

I didn't know there are perhaps ten million adoptees in the USA. I've met hundreds, both Indian and non-Indian. In 2013, I'm still meeting Lost Children and completing historical research for my third book, *Called Home*.

Every Indian reservation in North America has a story about missing lost children and future generations who carry the stigma of lost language and culture. If the Indian Child Welfare Act had been passed in the 1950s, my father Earl would have been contacted and he (or a relative) would have raised me. I never would have been lost or adopted.

Very few Americans know how the Indian Adoption Projects and Programs were an orchestrated act of genocide and ethnic cleansing. Many Indian friends remember when they were abducted as children, not babies, virtually erased from tribal rolls, not told their tribe or their family's name. This was legal until 1978 when the federal law (ICWA) was passed.

Like my adoptive mom and dad, families are very proud of their stories. To tell my story, I needed more than their story. I needed my own.

Trace A. DeMeyer is the author of *One Small Sacrifice: A Memoir* that details the little-known history of the Indian Adoption Project and the Indian Child Welfare Act; she includes her jaw-dropping journey to find her natural father and tribal relatives. A second book, an anthology *Two Worlds: Lost Children of the Indian Adoption Projects* was published in 2012, co-authored with Patricia Busbee. Her writing has been published in newspapers and journals in the U.S., Canada and Europe. Trace, a graduate of the University of Wisconsin-Superior, has received numerous news and feature writing awards. She lives in Massachusetts and blogs at Trace DeMeyer and Split Feathers.

Clarity Questions

1. Trace is listed as Earl's daughter in his obituary. For adoptees, this sense of public legitimacy is significant. What types of other signifiers have indicated to you your legitimacy, or lack thereof? If you're non-adopted, how do you feel about this claiming of family? Is it okay, even if adoptees have their "new families" by adoption?

2. Like many adoptees, Trace runs head-first into reunion. Of course, hindsight is 20/20. In the interest of helping future reunions, what, if anything, might Trace have done to protect herself from the dysfunction in her paternal first family, while remaining open to all of the new potential relationships?

3. Were you aware of the Indian Child Welfare Act and the reasons it was passed? What are your thoughts on the American Indian treatment at the hands of the U.S. Government?

Chapter 15

The Power of Story—

How Reunion Looks from Here

By Becky Drinnen

Story is where we came from. Story is where we're going. Story is what connects us and binds us to each other.

— Jeff Goins, "Power of Story"

Until I was nineteen, my life's story did not include my birth. I am adopted. My story started when I was three months old; on the day my parents drove to Cleveland, Ohio to pick me up. I love listening to their memories of this happy day. And I love seeing the pictures of me with my new family.

However, growing up adopted meant that what I

knew about the first three months of my life was confined to sterile details from a typewritten booklet prepared by adoption agency social workers. Details like this: *normal pregnancy, full term, labor 8 hrs. and easy, delivery low forceps and easy.* Sterile facts don't tell a story.

I have always known I was adopted; I don't remember being told. When I was younger, I didn't have a lot of questions. That changed when I was eight years old and my mom gave birth to my sister. By then I was old enough to understand how different my story was from my sister's. From that point on, I wondered more about the circumstances of my birth and the parents who were responsible for me walking this earth. At some level, I realized as a child that being adopted was not the normal course of things. I had questions, but I didn't question my right to know more about my origins.

My parents knew little to help me satisfy my curiosity. Mom remembered that my birth mother had red hair. So, every time I saw a woman with red hair, I looked at her features to see if I looked like her. I had so many questions. What does she look like? Does she ever think about me? Why did she give me up for adoption? Did she go to college? What did she like to do for fun? Did she like to read as much as I did? I believed I would never know the answers to these questions, and it made me sad.

My first experience with searching for birth family came well before the age of the Internet. When I was nineteen, I read a newspaper article about adoption. A sidebar in that article mentioned that, in Ohio, adult adoptees whose adoptions were finalized prior to January 1, 1964 could obtain a copy of their original birth certificate. My adoption was finalized in December 1963. My hands were shaking as I read those words and understood their impact. I didn't waste any time—the following week, I made the drive to Columbus to get a copy of those records.

In Columbus, I sat in a cold, sterile government office waiting for an obviously disapproving clerk to bring me my file for my review. I carefully looked through a few pages of legalese, searching for the good stuff. I had expected all the details about why I was placed for adoption, maybe a picture or two. Instead, I was looking at a copy of my amended birth certificate (the one with my adopted name and adoptive parents' names) along with the adoption decree that legally changed my identity. When I turned to the last page in that thin file— pay dirt. That last page was a copy of my original birth certificate. It looked just like the birth certificate I'd seen all my life, only the names were changed. She named me Laura. She had a name, too. And an age—she was twenty. The clerk asked if I wanted a copy. Really? Did she think I was going to commit this information to memory and go on? This information was MINE. Of course I wanted copies! I paid for my copies and drove home wondering what to do next.

I had something. And I had nothing. Pre-Internet

searches weren't easy. I had a name and address that had almost surely changed. I lived in a small town with a small library. I was a single mother, working a low-paying job with no benefits. My car was not exactly reliable. I couldn't afford to take time off to travel the state trying to track down my birth mother. Or to spend weeks researching in a larger library. I felt stuck. But determined. I did the only thing I knew to do: I unsuccessfully searched phone directories.

I pondered these small bits of information for months, wondering even more about this mystery mother who now had a name. I had a few more facts, important facts. However, what I had learned led to more questions. Why would a twenty-year-old woman think it necessary to give a baby up for adoption? Somehow, I had always imagined her to be younger—fifteen or sixteen. Why did she keep me for three months, then decide to place me for adoption?

During this time, I also wrote to the adoption agency that handled my adoption and requested the non-identifying information they were legally required to provide to me. I was disappointed with the sterile, bare facts contained in two short paragraphs. Physical descriptions of my parents, my maternal grandparents and a maternal aunt. Nothing that helped me understand who they were or why I was placed for adoption.

In time, I began a do-it-yourself search using the few tips I had been able to pick up in books I could access at my local library. I learned that vital records were public domain. I also learned that the State of Ohio would conduct a ten-year-range search for vital records. One by one, I requested documents that could lead me to my birth mother. First up, my birth mother's birth certificate. Fortunately, she had been born in Ohio, so I quickly had her birth certificate in my hands. I gained her birth date and the names of her parents.

I assumed she had married. So next I requested a marriage record for my mother. Once again, I was fortunate. She married in Ohio, so my first request resulted in a marriage license. Now I had a last name—if they had stayed married. More phone directory searches. No luck there. I had no idea where they lived currently and in the days before the Internet, there was no easy way to search multiple phone and city directories.

In an effort to trace her steps in time, I requested a birth certificate for a child born in the years after their marriage. They stayed in Ohio, so once again, my stamp and ten dollar check resulted in another birth certificate— this one for her second child, a son. This time, there was a father listed on the birth certificate. Other than knowing that I had a half-brother (I assumed this sibling had a different father), I didn't learn much more.

They seemed to stay put, so I hoped I would find my mother in Cleveland. A search of the Cleveland phone directory came up dry. No luck for my mother or her husband.

My luck was about to change. Soon after I received my brother's birth certificate, I mentioned my search to a friend. He had a police officer friend who was willing to take the information I had and search the Ohio BMV driver's license database. Bingo! A day later I had a current address and a phone number. She lived about a hundred miles from me. I would have eventually found this information, but that police officer certainly shortened my search!

Within a couple of days I was ready to make contact. I couldn't imagine that my birth mother wouldn't be interested in the baby she carried and placed for adoption twenty years ago.

I was wrong. Very wrong. Because a book I read on search and reunion recommended a third party making actual contact, a friend made "the call," with me listening in on an extension. In retrospect, I should have made the call myself.

She wasn't ready for contact. She listened to social workers and her parents and has never told husband or her other children about me. In the midst of raising teenagers, she was not at a place in her life where she was ready for contact with a firstborn child who remained a secret. Not ready is an understatement—she was hysterical during that short phone call. Her words are engraved in my memory—"What is she trying to do, ruin my life?"

She did take my phone number. Soon after, I received a phone call from my aunt, her sister. Her primary reason for contacting me was to elicit a promise from me to leave her sister alone. However, through my aunt, I was able to start putting together some pieces of my story. I got answers to some of my questions along with pictures of my birth mother, my grandparents and my three siblings.

The years were busy. I had work and a family to care for. I finished my bachelor's degree and my master's degree while working full-time. My birth family was never far from my mind, but, living in an adoption fog, I didn't feel I had the right to make further contact. My views began to change when the Internet and social media came along and opened my eyes about adoption-related issues. What I believed about adoptee search and reunion changed radically once I had access to more information.

My Facebook profile became the key to opening the floodgates of my adoption search. I had continued to hope that, once my birth mother got a little older, she would decide to get in touch with me. My aunt had my contact information—I assumed she and my birth mother had discussed her contact with me. By 2008, in my mid-40's, I was doubtful that my mother would ever reach out. But I wondered about my biological family. Every day.

Soon after joining Facebook, I spent a lunch hour searching for others I might know. On a whim, I typed in my mother's name. There she was, with a current picture. My hands shook; just like they did the day I first learned her name. I looked at photos. No pictures other than the profile picture. Her friend list, though, was golden. My three siblings, and some of their children, had Facebook profiles, too. Mostly private, so I didn't learn much. But I was able to see current pictures of my siblings. A window had opened just a little bit, but I was still on the outside.

I checked my birth family's profiles now and then (well, maybe more than now and then), always looking to see if there was anything new. I didn't learn anything significant until one Saturday afternoon I noticed that my brother and I had a mutual friend. My fingers went straight from the keyboard to my phone to find out how our mutual friend knew my brother. The surprising news she gave me—they worked together! Wow!

Twenty-some years after that first phone call to my mother, I was once again obsessed. My brother works eight miles from my house. With a friend of mine. Unbelievable. Thoughts of my birth family were now constant. I reached out on a couple of forums for advice. The responses were something I had never really considered: I didn't need my mother to reach out to my siblings. We are related and we are all adults. After much soul searching I realized that, as much as I am interested in my siblings, the person I really want to connect with is the woman who carried me under her heart for nine months before handing me over to strangers.

Over the next few weeks I worked up the nerve to make another call to her. The first time I called, rejection never crossed my mind. This time, I knew it was a very real possibility and I was terrified to make that call. Finally, my desire for answers about who I am and where I came from and about the woman who gave birth to me won out and I made the call. This time, after first denying I had reached the right person, she agreed to have a conversation with me. We talked for ninety minutes. Finally, I was having a conversation with the woman who gave me life.

I learned the answers to more of my questions. And more importantly, I felt an incredible sense of connection with her. She talked freely about her experience as a pregnant unmarried woman in the early 1960's. Her story mirrored those I have read about. Her choices were very few. So she did as she was told and placed me for adoption. I learned about my three siblings. She remembered the name she gave me. And she told me she has never forgotten me—and that she prays for me.

The impact of our conversation has deeply touched my life. With this conversation, pieces of the emptiness I felt when I wondered about the family I had never known started to be filled. I understood more of my story. I closed that first conversation hopeful that there would be more. Perhaps even a face-to-face meeting. Two years later, I have realized that she still lives in fear and denial of her past. I haven't given up hope, though I am realistic about the chances of her changing her mind. And I know her choices are about her. Not about me.

Maybe because of the details my mother told me

about my father, in the months after I spoke to my birth mother, my thoughts turned more frequently to my other unknown parent. Though my mother talked about my father, she did not tell me his name. His name wasn't on my birth certificate. I thought my mother held the key to his identity. After our conversation, I believed I would never learn his name. But I knew I had to try. Armed with all of the facts I had learned from my aunt, my mother and the non-identifying information from the adoption agency, I prepared to search once again in an attempt to give an unknown parent a name and a face.

The Internet made searching an entirely different experience. Instead phone calls and letters, I was able to search my way to answers from my home computer. With the help of genealogy tools such as an Ancestry.com subscription, a fellow adoptee with a Spokeo subscription, and online searches of newspaper archives, plus intuition and some luck, I learned the identity of my father in 2012. One more chapter of my story has begun to be written.

By finding my birth father, in some ways I feel like I have now learned everything I hoped for when I first began my search in the early eighties. I know the names of the two people responsible for giving me life. I also learned I have four more siblings—two brothers and two sisters. And I know a little bit about where I would have grown up if my parents had married.

In other ways I feel like I'm right back at the beginning. Once again I'm taking a risk to reach out to a birth parent who might reject me. This time, though, I'm reaching out knowing from experience that an accidental parent may not welcome me with open arms.

Within days of learning my birth father's name, I worked up my nerve to dial his phone number. I left a message. More waiting. I jumped every time my phone rang. Three days later, he called back. I began by asking if I could ask him for family history information. He was happy to answer my questions at first, but when I asked if he knew my mother, his tone changed. He ended the conversation telling me he would call me back. Not surprisingly, months later that call has not come. Once again, I find myself working up the nerve to make a phone call to one of the people responsible for giving me life.

Though I don't have any real closure with my birth parents, I have developed a relationship with birth family members that has brought me much joy. A wonderful twist to my story: searching for my birth father led me to a great uncle and aunt on my mother's side of the family. The experience with my aunt and uncle has been so much more gratifying than what I've experienced with my mother. They have welcomed me and provided me with much more knowledge of my ancestors than I ever expected. They have made me feel like a part of my birth family.

I've learned a lot in the years that have passed since I first searched for my birth family. One of the most important lessons has been learning to understand the difference between those things I can change and those things that are completely outside of my control.

All of the circumstances of my adoption were completely outside of my control. I had no say in any part of the adoption process. Even as an adult who has searched for and found birth parents, there are many circumstances that remain outside of my control.

Today, most importantly for me, that means acknowledging that I can't change that I was born in an era when unwed mothers were shamed. And I can't change that my birth mother has kept my existence a secret and doesn't want a relationship with me.

That means accepting that, though I have the right to know about my birth family, and they about me, I do not have the right to a relationship with them.

Is it what I prefer? No. But by accepting the truth that there are many circumstances about my adoptee status that I cannot control, my inner turmoil began to dissolve.

It's also funny how, once I accepted the truth that my birth mother's choices are about her and not about me, I began to see the choices I DO have open to me. By accepting what I can't control, I had room in my head for what IS possible:

She wouldn't tell me my father's name. I figured it out without her help.

I reached out to other birth family members (who

knew I existed) and I have discovered open hearts and open doors.

I started working on my family tree to learn about my family history. Their ancestors are mine, too. My birth parents can't change that.

I began to look outside of my own circumstances and began truly learning about how adoption affects others.

I have been able to channel my energy to an area of adoption where I can play a role in change: adoptee rights reform. I have access to my original birth certificate. Many adoptees do not. If my adoption had been finalized one month later, my original birth certificate would have been sealed. When I was focused on events I could not control, I was not able to look beyond myself. Now, I'm using my voice to help those who don't have the same rights I have and I am finding great joy in contributing to this cause. As a plus, the wonderful people in the adoption community I have connected with since I've started looking beyond myself have been a tremendous gift.

I have searched back when searching for birth family involved phone books, phone calls and musty books in the library. And I've searched when searches can be completed with a keyboard, search angels and Internet databases. There is no doubt that the Internet and social media has changed search. While much has changed in recent years thanks to the Internet, other areas of search have not evolved as quickly.

I, and many other adoptees, found at least some of those we searched for without the World Wide Web. It took longer, but it was possible to seek and find before the Internet. All of the information I used to find my birth father's identity would have existed without the Internet. However, I didn't have the time and the financial resources available to successfully complete that search. The gift of the Internet to those who search for birth family is ease of access. The Internet has made it possible for more people to have access to the information they need to search. There is no doubt that tools like Facebook, Ancestry.com, Spokeo, and Google make it easier to find those we seek.

Adoptees and birth parents still find that there are other roadblocks on the path to a successful reunion. Laws that control access to original birth certificates have been slow to change. Today, adoptees in ten states have easy access to their original birth certificates. The tide has begun to turn, but there is a lot of work to be done before the law treats all adoptees equally.

The Internet has also not changed the fact that some of those we seek don't want to be found. My experience has shown me that some reunion satisfaction can be found even if those we seek are not excited about being found. When I think about what reunion looks like to me today, it's not what I had hoped for. By accepting what I cannot change, I have given myself the gift of learning as much as possible about my biological family history and myself. I have satisfying relationships with a few extended family members. Because I searched, I know so much more of my story than I did on that day nearly thirty years ago when I first learned the name of the woman who gave birth to me.

If I had stayed immersed in the adoption fog, I would likely have stopped my search after that first contact with my mother. I found my path out of the adoption fog when I began connecting with other adoptees and first mothers on Internet forums, on Facebook and in the blogosphere. Thanks to the collective wisdom of those generous enough to share their experience as an adoptee or birth parent, there is a path for others to emerge from the fog.

I've come a long way in the past five years; I've gained just enough wisdom to know that it will not be smooth sailing through the rest of my journey. I'm very close to being ready to reach out to my birth father again. And at some point, I will once again contact my birth mother. And then there are my seven siblings. Four sisters and three brothers who do not know I exist. Four adult sisters and three brothers who have every right to know about their older sister and to choose whether or not they want a relationship, even if their parents do not. Today I'm not ready to reach out to my siblings.

I have no idea what other surprises are in store on the journey that began the day I drove to Columbus for a copy of my original birth certificate. I do know that what reunion looks like to me from this place in my life would be very different—and much less satisfying—if I had not accepted what IS and left room in my heart for what COULD BE.

I cannot imagine not knowing what I have learned about who I am and where I came from. It is not a fairytale with a storybook ending. It is a story full of the messiness of life. My story includes two sets of parents. I am the product of what both sets of parents have given me. I have always known the legacy my adoptive parents have contributed to my story. Now the legacy I inherited from my birth parents is part of my story too.

Update from the author:

Sometimes life changes so quickly. In the months between finishing this article and publication, much has changed. After a lot of soul-searching and conversations with a fellow adoptee, I chose to reach out to my birth father in person. That decision turned out to be one of the most terrifying and most satisfying events in my life. Today, five months after I first met my birth father, we are working at developing our relationship. I have also met other relatives, including two brothers and a sister. I have no idea where our relationships will go in time, but once again, I am learning that life is full of surprises. And I am learning more about where I came from than I ever dreamed possible.

Becky Drinnen is a baby-scoop-era adoptee who searched for and found her birth parents. Reunion with her birth father and family is a fresh, exciting development in her life. She is also an advocate for adoptee rights. Becky works in corporate America and loves her role as a wife, mom and grandma. In her free time, you'll find her immersed in genealogy research, reading a good history book, or enjoying the great outdoors. Becky blogs about adoption at Puzzles and Possibilities.

Clarity Questions

1. Becky was fortunate in that she was able to receive a copy of her original birth certificate, something which is only possible (at the time of this publication, 2014) in ten of the fifty U.S. states. Some adoptees see this information as a human rights matter: to have equal access to the true and accurate documentation of one's birth. What are your thoughts?

2. Becky talks a bit about her birth mom's sense of shame, and her birth father's unwillingness to call her back. What is the difference between privacy and secrecy? Do birth parents have a right to withhold medical information from their offspring? Do adoptees have a right to a relationship? From a policy standpoint how can sometimes competing desires be legislated? How does this factor into today's open adoptions?

3. When she mentions her adoption fog, Becky alludes to the fact that she has a lot going on in her life, besides her reunion search. What are your thoughts about the timing for search and reunion?

4. In discussing her path out of her fog, Becky talks a lot about what she can and cannot control. How could this idea apply to your own situation, or that of someone close to you?

Chapter 16

Coming Out of the Adoption Closet and Facing Secondary Rejection

By Laura Dennis

I exist.

It's go time. I'm "coming out."

Truly, I've been "out" as an adoptee for years. Hell, I published a book called *Adopted Reality*. Out of respect for my birth father's privacy, though, I changed his name and identifying details in the memoir. His wife knows I exist, but he never told his three kids.

After my birth father rejected me in a loud, aggressive fashion, I never contacted him again. But I always wanted to know my half-siblings. Furthermore,

I'm sick of my birth father holding a secret which isn't his to keep anymore. So, I decided to do something about it. This is an email I sent, and action taken to remedy what I see as an unjust situation (identifying details have been removed):

Dear Complete Stranger, Who is Also My Brother,

I'm a complete stranger to you. And yet, I'm your (half) sister.

I'm guessing this comes as a surprise. It's not a surprise for me; I've known who you are for more than ten years, but I waited to contact you until I was sure you were over eighteen.

Of course, the relationship between my birth mom and your dad was not meant to be. After I was born, your mom and dad got together, and soon enough, they had three beautiful children of their own.

In the meantime I was born, assigned to my new parents, and called Laura Dennis. It wasn't until I was 23, planning to get married, that I finally decided to search for my biological roots. In March 2001, I reunited with my birth mom. A few months later, I spoke several times with your dad. He acknowledged that he was my biological father. He mentioned that he had three children.

When I said, "They're my half-siblings," he replied, "I guess you could look at it that way."

Well, I do. I do look at it that way. I have three additional siblings, about whom I know extremely little.

Don't get me wrong. I love my adoptive family. They gave me unconditional love and support. I've had a good life. And yet. I have three *additional* siblings.

Why am I contacting you? Why am I potentially disrupting your life?

The best answer I can give you is, I would like to know you, and I would like you to know me.

I'm married, I have two children, aged three and five (your nephew and niece, actually!). I also know that when I was in my early 20's I was not interested in family "drama"; I was focused on socializing with friends and developing my career. I get it if you're not interested. I would be sad, but, I would understand. I would only ask that you please just let me know that you received this letter. Even if you don't want contact, just that you received it. Please.

I'm also sending a letter to your brother. I'm not sending one to your sister, because I believe she isn't eighteen yet, and I think it's best to respect her privacy until she is an adult. (That doesn't mean that I don't want to know her, though!)

I am 99.9% sure that I am your half-sister. I found you through a mutual friend of my birth parents. I hope I can be "found" back.

Love, Laura

Almost immediately, the eldest brother blocked me on Facebook. My younger brother has not responded. It's been almost a year.

In the early weeks, I was sad and confused, but also at peace. I tried, I outed myself, and I'm still okay. I look at the photo of the younger brother and it's bittersweet … because he looks so much like my own (non-adopted) son. They even have the same haircut.

I've really wanted to write about this secondary rejection. It happens more often than people realize, and comes in a variety of forms. It's important for the non-adopted world to realize that adoption secrets still exist. People are hurting because of them. Nevertheless, I've been reluctant to post this story, and I asked myself: *Why?*

I realized that I was keeping quiet because I hoped that if I remained a "nice, grateful, compliant adoptee," I wouldn't be rejected *again.* Maybe, if I waited long enough and patiently enough, my birth father and his family would realize I'm loveable and would respond to me.

Then, I decided to take this secondary rejection and raise it one loud adoptee. This, right here, is the adoptee trump card: I'm out. I'm adopted. Truly, I'd love to hear from you, but I won't be crying any tears if and actually, *when,* I don't. You may think I'm crazy, you may want nothing to do with me, but you know what? I exist. I *won't* be quiet. I. am. still. here.

More importantly, I have plenty of people who like and even love me. I choose to focus on them.

Clarity Questions

1. There's rejection, secondary rejection, tertiary rejection, and so on. How can adoptees minimize these feelings, these emotional triggers of abandonment, rejection and feelings of unworthiness? If you've experienced this type of rejection, do you feel as if you never should have reached out?

2. Facebook, social media and google searches have made it a lot easier to reach out and connect. What are the potential pitfalls and downfalls to easier, faster and cheaper access?

Chapter 17

Full Circle Thanksgiving

By Samantha Franklin

Reunion has brought so many conflicting emotions over the years, especially surrounding the holidays. Truly like trying to untangle a ball of yarn without knowing its beginning or end.

For many years after reunion, I would reluctantly turn down invitations each holiday, feeling a strong obligation to my adoptive family. Feeling extreme guilt for even trying to see my family of birth "around" the holiday—so torn. Wondering and longing through feelings of self-doubt and paralyzing covetousness of those in my first families who never lost their place. Not knowing who I was or where I belonged.

This flowed over even into celebrations around my son. Birthday parties, which are supposed to be joyous times of fellowship and fun became so stressful that I would avoid planning them. So sad. Who would I invite? I wanted everyone there but couldn't stand the thought of trying to merge these segregated and conflicting families in the same place. Holidays brought up buried pain of separation, ownership, and confusion.

Finally walking through the pain of grief unlocked my ability to feel and embrace the love that my family(ies) were trying to show. The love I so wanted to be able to feel and embrace and return.

I want to thank God for bringing me through those crashing emotions of reunion. To a more quiet acceptance and embrace of who I am and who my family is. Amazing.

Yesterday was really nice. My mom was in my home again for the first time since April, when she fell and was hospitalized and then moved to a senior center. My son was so excited he climbed all over her, even in her wheelchair. Her personality is amazingly positive and such an inspiration to me, for her to be able to weather so many months of health issues and change. My first father dropped by right when we were putting Thanksgiving lunch on the table, and I so enjoyed seeing him and sharing this special day and lunch—just being together means so much.

He had not seen my mom for many years (the families spent more time "together" during the infant stage of reunion—I feel like the beginning of "my" reunion was more for them than for me—so shy and emotionally numb).

I didn't beat myself up emotionally this time for letting my mom see the heartfelt emotion of hugs and kisses between my first father and us. Maybe he is opening up more because I am.

Then, last night I got to be an adult (not just "Mommy") for a few hours at Thanksgiving dinner hosted by my first mother's brother and sister (my aunt and uncle). We sipped white wine and feasted on turkey and dressing (yet again) all evening, enjoying each other's company, getting caught up on our lives and telling stories of growing up in Tulsa (separated, yet within blocks of each other our whole lives). Uncle Ron lives on Reservoir Hill just north of downtown—with a spectacular view of the city lights, the moon and the stars, and a crackling outdoor fireplace.

I am so blessed to be reunited with my entire family of birth. The rich diversity and YEARS of getting to know them, and the strong love that has grown. I have a beautiful heritage of faith in my family, by both adoption and birth. And also great diversity. Jewish on my father's side, and my first mother's side includes a beloved uncle by marriage who grew up in the Middle East. And yet another from Guatemala!

My young cousins, Sean and Hanna, who I was privileged to watch grow up and grew close to these past twenty years have a beautiful dual-heritage, which they are learning to embrace and be proud of. We talked about the importance of family and how we can learn so much from the strong family traditions and customs of other cultures—how they stay close throughout their lifetimes and help each other through hard times. How they value the little things in life, without the distraction of the "rat race" we all seem to battle in America.

I am finally more complete in my identity and families now, and am so thankful. Still growing so much and overcoming. But thankful.

Clarity Questions

1. What was your reaction to Samantha describing feelings of "self-doubt and paralyzing covetousness" when it comes time to spend holidays or special occasions with her first family?

2. Have you or an adoptee you know been able to come to a "quiet acceptance and grace through … faith"? Why or why not?

Part 4

Coming to Terms with the Adoption Paradox,

Or,

It's Complicated

Chapter 18

The Happy Adoptee and the Reunited Adoptee Sharing the Same Body

By Gaye Vale

Time to move in.

Slowly I follow my brother, feeling all eyes on me. My husband and children are with me, my strength.

"Sit here. You should be up here," my brother's partner says.

Smile. Slight shake of the head. "No," I say, "That's your place. I'll be right here."

My sister turns and smiles, "You okay?"

I nod and smile, holding back the tears.

The celebrant starts to read the words I helped write, the words that give me the history I was not part of, the words that make me feel the loss even more deeply.

And then the music. It is her music. It is music I never heard play. It is music I didn't sing and dance along to with her.

The photos. At times it is a mirror I am looking into and at others, a record of all that was and everything that I missed. No words are necessary. Her beauty and strength speak loudly, and her smile lights up the room. There she is as a young girl. Look, she's with her first born son. Now she's with her baby girl, who she adores and has raised into the most amazing woman. Another person enters the frame—a daughter lost but now found. Me.

There are smiles. They smile down at me as I cry. I cry for the pain she went through. I cry for the pain I went through. I cry for the times lost. And I cry for the happiness finding her has brought me. And I cry that she is now gone.

Tears were also shed on December 14, 1961, the day I was born six weeks premature and the day that I was removed from my mother. Her tears should have been tears of joy. Instead, they were cries of despair and agony at not being even allowed to see her baby daughter, let alone to hold her.

They were the tears of a baby not allowed to be held close by the woman who had carried her all these months, scared, lonely cries born of the purposeful separation of two who had been one for so long.

My mother's tears, I've been told, did not end when after another six weeks, she gave up trying to get to her daughter, and she had no choice but to succumb to the pressure on her to make the separation permanent. But to survive, she had to find ways of dealing with the emptiness she was left with and the fact that she would never see Catherine again.

As for me in 1961? Well, the tears didn't last forever. There was no use. I did not "thrive," as they say, for the first six weeks. I was alone in a hospital and no more than another task, I imagine, to those employed to care for me. It wasn't until six weeks after my birth that I left the hospital to join my adoptive family. I've been told that I spent the next six months crying and screaming, a sickly child. My adoptive mother shared this story numerous times, I still hear it today, how my distress and poor condition was caused by no one caring for me in the hospital. That is it. That's where my life begins, with a visit to the hospital by my adoptive parents, with them "choosing" me. "You can't leave her here," said my adoptive father, and they didn't.

Don't get me wrong, my adoptive parents were genuine and caring. They loved me as their own, and raised me to have strong community values and respect for others. They taught me to value the person above all possessions or positions. They were generous with what little they had and shared with their children, their biological son and their two adopted daughters, a loving relationship on all levels.

What they couldn't give me, no matter how much they loved me, was my identity. I could not look in the mirror and see a family connection. Nor could their love remove my constant need to seek approval and affirmation—otherwise they might not want me here anymore. Nor could it stop me from wondering why my mother didn't want me, or making up stories about who my mother was and how one day she would come back for me. The constant need to "be good" was exhausting, and occasionally the facade was broken. I did many negative things—some of them so childish, that it is embarrassing, both now and at the time. But I couldn't stop myself from behaving like that. I was scared. I was different. I was worthless. I was unwanted. I was a fraud. I was alone. The child in me is still fighting those thoughts. The realization of this came much later. At the time, I really didn't know why I was doing these things.

But I get ahead of myself. So when did I find out I was adopted? I remember the word bandied around a lot as I grew up, primarily by adults who would look down at me with a sweet, knowing smile while discussing this "thing." But of course at this stage, "adoption" or "adopted" could have meant any number of things: small for her age; terribly shy; or different from her brother, maybe. Whatever it meant, if I took on that shy stance with little eyes daring to glance from my bowed head partly hidden by my adoptive mother's skirt... if I then smiled timidly, everyone seemed happy. All was good. Everything must have been okay, because so many of these people commented on how lucky I was. If they said it, and if my adoptive mother agreed, then it must be so. I was lucky, all because I had managed to find my way into the lives of my adoptive family. I should be grateful. I learned to wear "lucky and grateful" as my adoptee uniform.

Then some of my cousins started mentioning it, asking questions such as, *How does it make you feel to be adopted?* and *Where is your "real" mother?* They asked these questions, but never in front of the adults. It was something only discussed down the backyard or when we children were alone in our room. It had to be something shameful the way it was spoken about secretly. I understand now that my cousins asked mostly out of curiosity. But it hurt. It was scary, because if they knew, then everyone did. But if everyone knew, then why hadn't my adoptive mum and dad told me about it?

We shifted suburbs and schools when I was in Grade 4. The house was worse than a "renovator's delight." My father even fell through the front stairs on the first day we were there. But this was home, and instead of running the streets we had the run of the mudflats across the road. It was kids heaven from that perspective. And I thought father's heaven too, as it was only a couple of years after we arrived that my adoptive father took up fishing. It was about 20 years later that I finally was let in on the secret that he actually hated fishing, but hated sitting at home in our renovator's delight even more. It turns out he was unable to do the work he knew needed doing because of his angina. Doesn't seem like a big deal, but it is just another example of the half-truths or lies that make up the story of me.

Your mother didn't love you or want you, and that's why you're adopted.

Kids can be mean, and this is what confronted us at our new school. Now, although I had heard the word before, I had never experienced it in such a negative way that undermined the "lucky" connotation it had held previously. My adoptive parents did love me and never wanted any harm to come to me, so what these kids had said must be true. My adoptive mum and dad never talked to us about it. I figured this must be because they knew it would hurt us to know that we weren't wanted and weren't loved by the woman who was our real mother. With all the cowardice I could muster, I made my younger adopted sister ask the questions. *What does adopted mean?* and *Are we adopted?...* Finally we were both told we were adopted, we had different mothers who couldn't look after us, and mum and dad were so lucky to be given that chance. They loved us and we were their little girls. Done. That was the last conversation about adoption that I had with my adoptive mother and father for at least ten years. It simply wasn't discussed.

We all experienced grief when my adoptive father died when I was ten years old. The grief of my adoptive mother was extreme. So whatever I was feeling, I tried to hide it because she was in so much pain. I was scared that if I caused too much trouble, now that it was only her, I might be sent back. To where I had no idea. And why I would think that—it definitely was not through anything that she or my father had ever said or done. It was just there, in my head and was part of my reality. So I bottled it all up.

The sadness I felt at losing my adoptive father.

The fear of being sent away and having no one.

The unfairness I felt at losing yet another parent, after having been taken from my first mum and dad.

I put a lid on it all and got on with being good, publically at least. I was sent to a Catholic girls school to be a lady (money wasted I still believe). I did well at school, played sports, got a part time job to help with the money, ended up as school captain and was offered a place at university. Yes, life was good. And I was grateful.

Adoption was not something I thought of a lot during my high school years, and definitely something that didn't get a lot of conversation space. I had a lid on it. If I did think about it, I wondered why, and I thought of not being good enough. I was the happy child of my adoptive mother, who then grew into a happy young adult. Or that is what I told myself and the image I presented.

In reality, the early miscarriage I had at the age of 20—just before my wedding, and being pregnant with my firstborn at the age of 21 tell a different story. I was desperate for love and desperate for a family, to create the bloodline that I had been denied. At that time I didn't realize this, but looking back with what I now know, it is so obvious. Yes. I knew my lines (or lies) very well, so well that even I believed them. Mind you, I was very insecure, always waiting for my boyfriend (then husband) to leave me because ... I think deep down I knew I was not good enough to love. I was always scared that I would lose what I loved and was waiting for it to happen.

So what happened to the lid? Well, there were occasions when it had to lift a little. The first time was when I was 21 and pregnant with my firstborn. Because of the earlier miscarriage I was scared of losing another baby, so I contacted the Department of Families and requested my "natural mother's" (the terminology I used at the time) medical information so I could give this to my doctor. That's all I wanted, and I couldn't see that it would be a problem. Wrong. That information was not available. But, apart from dislocated hips, my daughter was healthy. The lid was put back in place.

Then in 1992 the laws changed and I could apply for identifying information and my birth certificate (which I could have if I paid the fee! They took it from me in the first place and now wanted me to pay for it.). I now had my mother's name and began to think about searching. I did a little bit, but really didn't know how to and gave up. In 1996 the lid was lifted, and again for medical reasons. I was finding it hard to fall pregnant with my new husband and thought I'd see if I could get any further by searching. I discovered that medical information was available with "non-identifying information." So I hadn't asked for the right thing and would need to lodge a further application. The barriers put in our way— unbelievable.

So what information did I now have? Well, she was 21 when she had me and there were no other births recorded. *Wow. The same age as when I had my daughter.* She was married but separated for three years. *That threw me a little. So young to get married initially. And before I had this piece of the puzzle through the "non-identifying information," I had wasted so much time searching for her under her married name. Fail!* She was five-feet, one-and-a-half inches. *That's exactly my height and I always claim that extra half an inch! Smiling to myself over that one!* Blue eyes. *So have I.* She lived at Cribb Island. *That's Brisbane isn't it? Have to check the street directory. Maybe she's still there.* Father, unknown. *Wonder why? Obviously not on the scene. I am sure she wanted me but couldn't look after me.* Father's height—tall. *I certainly didn't take after him that way then.*

Really there was so little information provided that part of me was dying inside thinking that was it. That is all I am worth. No medical history because in those days, apparently, they didn't always record it. (I'd wager they didn't bother to record it for babies like me—those with the "for adoption" label.) And where was she? I think part of me expected to get the information and then make a phone call and that would be that. I would know who I was, I would know the story of why I wasn't kept, and I would know the story of how she really felt. Unrealistic I know, but another blow all the same.

Then again, there was enough about my mother for me to start to make a connection with her. I began to do searches of phone books and on the Internet. I wrote to some people who may have been relatives but got no replies. That I didn't like doing. I didn't tell people I was adopted. I tried to hide that so as not to have to talk about it. If I had to talk about it, I knew deep down that maybe the script I lived by might be disturbed. And then where would I be?

So the on-again off-again pursuit of who I was continued for a number of years. I'd get a spurt of longing when the lid was lifted, and then it would go down again, but creep open at a time I was not expecting it.

I certainly was not expecting what followed. I didn't know many other adoptees, because no one spoke of it. The one person I did speak with—my adoptive sister, was in the same "adoptee happy space" as I was: not seeing a need to search. But in the course of my work, I met this woman—older than I, who was chatting with colleagues about seeing her sisters. She showed me the photos of that meeting. I made the appropriate observation of how much of a resemblance there is between them. She explained that it was the likeness that totally amazed her, too. She was adopted out and had only just found her family—well, they had found her—and how great it was. The only sad bit was that her mother had died a number of years earlier, and she had never had the opportunity to reunite with her.

Now remember, I was in my "adoptee happy place"—probably the most settled and content I had ever been. I had a loving second husband, three great children, two still at school, a good job and a great group of friends and neighbors. I no longer felt inferior, undeserving and unworthy. I learned I didn't have to be good all the time, and my pattern of over-achieving shifted to one of doing a good job in whatever I took on. I also had my adoptive mother living with me, as she had major health issues and could no longer live without assistance. This wasn't easy but in many ways I felt I owed it to her as her adoptive daughter and we were rewarded when, after getting her condition under control, the smile returned to her face.

So I surprised myself when I revealed to this woman, a new colleague, that as an adoptee, I thought that her story was just beautiful. She then spelled out what I had to do. She told me to make sure that I did not leave it until too late to meet my mother. That whatever her reaction was, and whether or not it was an ongoing relationship, at least I'd be able to fill in the gaps. Even being able to look at a photo and see the resemblance is something that every adoptee needs, whether they know it or not. But what had happened to my colleague—to get so close and to find out her mother had died, was so sad for her and so hard to accept, for the both of us.

That night, after the husband and children were tucked safely in bed, I typed my mother's name and pressed "search." I had done this at different times and found nothing. So you may imagine my surprise when this listing on OzReunion came up:

Name: Unknown

Date of Birth: Mid-to-late December 1961

Town of Origin: Brisbane

Notes: I am looking for my sister who was born at Royal Women's Hospital – Brisane late 1961. I don't have much information to go on and your birth father was not listed. Mum cannot remember your exact date of birth as she suffered a nervous breakdown after your adoption and her memory has blanked out the date. Would love to meet you, so please take a chance and make contact.

I got no response to my email, so I called. It was a Monday morning. No answer. I left a message. Half an hour later I was talking with my sister. She was very suspicious at first, but I had the correct details, including the name my mother gave me. I emailed the documents I had to her, and from there she organized to meet me for lunch later that week. The week couldn't pass quickly enough. I was a bit anxious—more about what she'd think of me than anything else. There's that low self-esteem rearing its ugly head again.

My resemblance to my mother was what blew my sister away, and it wasn't only the way I looked, but my mannerisms, the way I spoke and looks that I gave her. My sister's resemblance to a younger me, and her life events almost mirroring mine (apart from the adoption of course), blew me away. What impressed me was her desire to protect our mother, who was not all that well. My sister wondered how she was going to balance our mother's desires with my need to meet her. And she did it well. We exchanged background information in writing, as well as photos, and she walked this journey with our mother.

Then the day came.

I was nervous driving to the café where we were to meet—my mother, my sister and I. I will be late for my own funeral, there is no doubt. But not on this day. Checking my hair and straightening my clothes, yes, I was nervous. Finally I was going to find out who I really was, nearly 48 years after I was born. But once I was there and sitting with my mother and sister, there were no tears. The nervousness disappeared. I was where I needed to be. I was where I should be. I was finally complete. My sister, on the other hand, was extremely nervous, worried and scared, I imagine, that she had started something without knowing just how it would play out or where it would end. My reunion progressed so quickly that I think my sister and I had to draw breath on occasion as we worked out where to go next, emotionally speaking. Given her age and illness, both of us tried to protect our mother along the way. But our mother left neither of us, nor her son, in any doubt that this was good and what she wanted.

She told me later that one morning after our first meeting she announced to the bus load of "oldies" (she didn't consider herself old) that she had found her daughter. She was rather a private person and the fact that she made such a public statement shows just how happy and proud she was to finally be reunited with her daughter.

On the first Mother's Day that we were together, she met my adoptive mother for the first time. The two spent a long time chatting and thanking each other for what they each did. She met all her grandchildren and had a real soft spot for my husband. She was a proud woman with much to be proud of. She was also a kind-hearted person, a bit on the gruff side, as a result of the hurt she carried. What I saw was my mother and what a beautiful person she was.

My mother was so gracious and generous with her information at that first meeting and subsequently. She hadn't wanted to give me up. She didn't have a choice. She was single with no income and no family support. Her brother probably would have taken me, but his first son was born a couple of days after me, and they couldn't do it. Social services had told her that she would never keep the child and she should do what's right, or they would come and take the baby. (Her fear of social services haunted her for the rest of her life, constantly living in fear that her children would be taken from her.) She never got to hold me or even to see me, but she named me Catherine, as that was the name she'd always wanted to give her first daughter. She was told that I was going to go to a very good home, a doctor's family. That I would be well looked after and cared for by this family that could give this baby so much more than she could ever hope to. (*They told my adoptive parents that I had come from good stock—my mother was a doctor. Lies from the start.*) She was just so happy that I had a good life, and I was happy. She didn't have a choice, and as I was to find out, neither did so many other women from 1950 to 1980 in Australia.

The reality is that I was "lucky" enough to be born during the era of forced adoptions in Australia. The stories are horrific, and the impact on generations of mothers, fathers and children immeasurable. Many mothers, like mine, were stripped of their parental rights and put in the situation of having no choice. Some query how that could be and why then did they sign the adoption papers? My reply—if it was something they were doing willingly then why was it that so many of them never even saw their babies? They were taken from them and their requests to see their babies denied by the doctors and nurses. Some were drugged at the time of birth. Others had pillows placed over their heads so that they could not see their baby. No one spoke to these women, except to tell them they could not look after the baby and not to worry, they could have other babies later when they were married. I don't know the full story of the inhumane and unethical treatment my mother got. I do know that her labor lasted for three days, and as she tells it, no one came near her or helped her. She was simply left—alone, in pain and scared. She may have been drugged, as she remembers little of the birth except that her baby was taken and she was not allowed to see her.

Much work has been done by first mothers groups to have the government admit what happened admitted to them, and their children. A number of Australian states have issued their own governmental apologies. After years of work, a national apology was issued by the then Prime Minister Julia Gillard in March 2013. The long-awaited apology followed the huge response to the 2012 publications of the "National Research Study on the Service Response to Past Adoption Practices," conducted by the Australian Government through the Australian Institute of Family Studies (Research Report No. 21), and the Federal Government's Senate Inquiry into the Former Forced Adoption Policies and Practices.

I was one of the 823 adoptees who participated in the survey that contributed to the Research Report.

Overall, it is quite a disturbing read. I didn't fully understand that as an individual I could contribute to the Senate Inquiry (head-in-sand again I'd say), but a huge number of adoptees (not just first mothers) participated in that also. Most definitely, I was no longer "the only adoptee I knew;" I was part of a huge number of grown adults across Australia who had been denied their heritage, denied access to their records, denied their mother's love, and denied genetic information that would support their ongoing health and wellbeing.

I thought then that one of the best ways of honoring my mother was to get a copy of the National Apology. I registered my mother and myself for copies. She was getting so ill (dementia is a devastating illness for the person and their family), I was unsure it would mean anything to her. But I was going to get it anyway.

Until this point I had all but ignored the historical reality of the extent of what had happened in my country. Being isolated and not involved in any support groups or associations linked to adoption, I was the happy adoptee with no need of her past. I finally realized that the biggest loser in this game of denial was me. What I didn't fully understand was that I was about to pay a very heavy cost for my decades of denial.

My mother passed away in April 2013. Her copy of the National Apology arrived the day of her funeral. I placed it on her casket. I was lucky to find her and lucky to have her for three years and five months. But I weep from my very core when I think of the years lost as I lived the lie that accompanied the happy adoptee facade. The lie of not needing to know, of not needing to find my mother, my history and my identity.

Why is it that the happy adoptee and the searching adoptee can't share the same space? I think it goes back to the start of the story of adoption for me—how special I was to be chosen, how lucky to be part of this new family, and how *grateful* I have to be for being special and lucky. However, if the lies were dropped and some honesty prevailed, there is no reason why the happy adoptee and the searching adoptee cannot coexist. After all, my mother and my adoptive mother found friendship. So what was I so scared of all those years?

Her favorite song, the music I didn't share with her—listening, singing, dancing all those years—played as we left the chapel. It was a song by country and western singer Slim Dusty, called, *Looking Forward Looking Back* ... "Got a long way left to go."

Although I may not have known the song, I now knew some of the challenges my mother faced during her life and can understand why this was her favorite song. I like to think of it as wisdom from a mother to her children, to both her daughters and her son, her final message of hope. And it is true. To look forward, to continue my journey, I have had to look back and sort out the lies and half-truths. I must finally be able to experience the attachment that was denied to me as a baby, and I have come to know my genetic history. I need to accept the trauma that was imposed on both my mother and me. Only through looking back can I truly look forward to creating my songs with my voice, and not with the programmed and learnt voice of my childhood. I am still working on it. Although I do believe that I have found out much of what my real story is, there are gaps that will always be there, because I left it until too late to find my mother. With her being in the very early stages of dementia, it was not the time to be taking her back to such a painful part of her life. As my uncles, brother and sister all say, "It is such a pity you didn't show up earlier. You would have loved her."

Well, I do love her—I love her because she gave birth to me.

I love her for not being beaten by a system that did not provide the protection and support it should have and did not give her the basic human rights she was entitled to.

I love her because she went on to share her love with my brother and sister.

I love her because she was waiting for me to find her and welcomed me with open arms.

I love her because even though she was ill, she gave fully of herself to me in those three-and-a-half short years we had together.

I love her for saying right until the end, "I can't

believe you are here." Right to the end, my mother let me know that she never gave up on me.

Gaye Vale was born and raised in Brisbane, Australia. She is married with three children, two girls aged 30 and sixteen, and a son aged ten, and she recently welcomed her second grand-child to the clan. Gaye worked in a variety of roles until following her childhood dream to be a teacher. She taught high school for almost a decade, including a year in London. Gaye has been an activist for women's rights for many years and was one of the founders of the women-only political party, the Australian Women's Party in the late 1990s. Gaye now works as a union organizer assisting and supporting school employees, and as her defogging progresses, hopes to gain her voice as an advocate for adoptee rights. Connect with her via email at gayevale@icloud.com.

Clarity Questions

1. Gaye talks a lot about the lid she kept on her curiosity. How it would lift, but then she would stuff the

contents back down and forget about searching. She attributes her reluctance to search coming from fear of not appearing grateful, low self-esteem and deep seeded denial.

How can adopted children benefit from the wisdom of adult adoptees? What can be done to break this cycle of fear and denial?

2. Is it possible for the happy adoptee and the searching/reunited adoptee to share the same space in one person?

Chapter 19

When a Reunion Isn't a True Reunion

By Deanna Doss Shrodes

The unknown.

It haunted me most over the years as an adoptee.

Who and where did I come from?

Why wasn't I raised with my original family?

Was there no one, absolutely **no one**, in the large maternal family I come from, who could step up and care for me, to keep me with the family?

Why was it determined that I would be better off raised with strangers outside the family, and not my kin?

For years I fantasized that if I could just meet my original mother, all of my questions would be answered. The unknown would suddenly be known. Leaving the prison of secrecy would finally be a reality for me after almost three decades of life.

Living with so many unanswered questions was the most difficult aspect, although I almost never spoke of it. Like many—perhaps even most—adoptees, I kept all of my feelings about this to myself. There's an unwritten rule that we're just supposed to be okay with all of this and maintain a thankful heart just because we are alive.

One thing I have sensed from countless adoptees is that it's hard sometimes to overflow with thankfulness for being alive when being alive hurts so much. And, most people don't understand what we need to heal and in fact, tell us we don't have a right to it nor will they give it to us.

The Long and Winding Road

Mine was a rocky road to the actual reunion with my original mother. The first time she had any contact regarding me as an adult was with a confidential intermediary through the reunion program of the adoption agency that I was placed with.

Very long story short—she said no.

And I cried myself to sleep for two years.

During the day I was managing two babies who are a year apart in age, as well as holding a demanding position of staff pastor of a mid-size church. I held myself together during the day for the sake of my husband, children and church and at night I would sob until I was wrung out like a dishrag. There were times I sensed I was going to sob and lose control during the day and I'd quickly get to a private place where no one would have to witness my pain. After two years of crying and hearing from God in prayer, I decided to continue searching and ultimately approach her myself.

I believe every human being has a right to look into the eyes of the two people they originate from, at least once. And if they are not still alive—a name and a photo of the persons they come from. I don't believe they have a right to bombard them after that with further contact, to stalk or harass them. I do however, believe that if you birth a child—it's the humane thing, the kind thing—yes, the right thing to do, to give them a face-to-face with you at least once, if they request it.

My plan was to meet her once, say what I had to say, give her a journal I had written for her over the years and then ask her if I could have one photo to remember her by if she never wanted to see me again. I took a camera just in case she was not willing to part with a photo.

Upon finding out my mother's name and address, I drove the eight hour trip to knock on her door unannounced and meet her.

Yes, it was the scariest thing I ever did.

Yes, my legs were like Jello walking up to her door.

Yes, it was extremely awkward at first.

Our conversation that night resulted in what is now a twenty year relationship with she and my step father, and (half) brother and sister.

Even though I entered into an active relationship with the maternal side of my family, I learned quickly that reunion doesn't magically solve everything. Something inside me did settle down to a degree once I met my mother and siblings. But so much never settled down.

Many who are not adopted fail to realize that **adoption is not a thing of the past for adoptees**. You wake up adopted, each day—for the rest of your life. Even in reunion! I have been told, "You aren't adopted... you *were* adopted. That is past. Now, you just need to leave the past behind, and move on." The fact is that I will always be adopted—even with the knowledge and relationship with my maternal family—reunion does not change that I am still an adoptee. And, many of my questions go unanswered.

The Missing Piece

At peace with the knowledge of who my mother, sister and brother were—and my active relationship with them, there was still part of me missing.

My natural father.

Twenty years of reunion on my maternal side passed, without knowing who my original father was.

My mother made it clear from the first night of our reunion; he wasn't a subject up for discussion. On the night of our reunion she told me my father was Greek, in fact she referred to him as a "Greek God." I was told that

I looked like him. She expressed obvious distain for him, saying that he did not acknowledge nor help her with the pregnancy. She inferred in our talk that night that he refused to believe that I existed. For all these years my husband has jokingly said, "I can assure everyone she exists. I pay her bills!"

I was so grateful to be in relationship with my natural mother and siblings that I did whatever it took to keep the peace and not keep asking about my father, though my questions churned inside.

It was hard for me to mount up the courage to go there again. After everything I went through to gain not only knowledge of, but an active relationship with my maternal family, I didn't want to ruin it.

My natural (half) sister had inquired over the years, asking my mother about my first father.

She believed that it was very important for me to know.

And, she told our mother that she felt I needed to know the truth.

Yet this part of my history was a vault—sealed up tight.

When dealing with the subject of a father, mothers need to realize that it's not just a part of her history but the adoptee's history too. The mother and daughter or son are co-owners of this history. Observing my own family dynamics, as well as many others, shows me that many others do not realize that someone else is also the rightful co-owner of this information.

The years were going by and I realized my original father, if still alive, was not getting any younger. Time was running out, to find him. I try and try to imagine what he looks like. What his voice sounds like. Apparently I favor him, this Greek God.

I assumed that searching out faces in public places to find features like mine would leave when I reunited with my mother. It doesn't. I still stare into men's faces everywhere, especially ones who are elderly Greek men, focusing in on their unique features, wondering if they are my original father. I try to look away nonchalantly, if they notice I am staring at them.

The Great Rift Valley

I've been to the Great Rift Valley in East Africa, and stood over the vast expanse. I've stared down and imagined what it would be like to fall from there, and taken many photos of its beauty. Even so, I've emotionally experienced a much more traumatic fall than what I've ever envisioned as a possible fall into the Great Rift Valley.

I mounted the courage to ask my mother for my father's name.

Not only did she decline and say she wasn't willing to give me his name, ever, although she most certainly knows who my father is... but it resulted in a horrible falling out. It was the Great Rift of our relationship, creating a huge valley of pain between us.

The breach was so traumatic, the words spoken so painful; I ended up going to therapy to be able to move forward. I worked for four months on healing for me, and on mending our relationship.

When the rift between us first occurred, I would often ruminate with my circle of friends that, "I never asked her for anything before... only my father's name. I've expected nothing of her... and now... this!!!" Upon asking my mother to verify this, she even agreed with me that I had never asked her for anything and said I had been a blessing for twenty years.

Truth be told while I didn't ask her for anything, I came to realize that I did have unspoken expectations.

After she agreed to come into active relationship with me, I was looking to my natural mother for what I perceive as motherly attributes: unconditional love, acceptance, understanding, the willingness to do **anything** within one's power to take away a child's pain. These are all things I would give and do for my kids, and so naturally I just thought, "This is what my mother will do for me... "

And that's not what happened.

It seemed so simple, this asking for my mother to give me two words, a first and last name.

I wasn't asking her to see him, talk to him, or have anything to do with him. I only wanted his name and I would take it from there.

I chose to go the route of DNA testing, with three companies. At first when I let her know I had chosen this path, she told me our relationship would be over if I pursued it. She later changed her mind but our relationship never healed although I did make an effort.

Four months after the rift between us, my mother was diagnosed with cancer. She died just two months later. I never received his name from her. She took her secrets to the grave, just as she promised me she would. What resulted was not only a process of healing I had to embark on to move forward from her death, but I also needed to heal from her refusal to give what I needed most.

My dreams of reunion were many.

I wanted to finally get out of what is known by adoptees as the "Ghost Kingdom."

To have all my questions answered about my history.

To know my natural parents' identities.

I am over twenty years out from reunion, and this has not happened.

Disappointment in Reunion

A lot is said about "angry adoptees." Frankly, the anger is justified in that we have not received basic human rights extended to those who are not adopted.

I would not describe myself as an angry adoptee, yet I would describe myself as a disappointed one. Therapy has been invaluable to bring me to a place of peace and joy in my daily life, particularly with the family my husband and I have created, and our many friends.

I could wallow in my adoptee-disappointment daily and make no personal progress. This would be very easy to do as some days it's overwhelming. But I've chosen to burn the disappointment, and yes, some days the anger, as fuel for the journey.

My disappointment burns as fuel to light the fire of my legacy. I'm determined to live differently than those who have gone before me.

I spent my mother's final hours with her at hospice, having ample time alone with her. I never brought up the subject of my father during that time, as I didn't want to put any stress on her in last moments, not to mention she was unable to speak. However when we had the private family viewing before she was cremated, I went to the casket alone and shared my feelings, in an act of closure for me. I know she wasn't there—only the shell of her body was there, but for me it felt like she was present, because her body lay before me. I quietly stood over her casket and declared who I was and why. I shared with her about decisions I've made for my life, influenced heavily by decisions she made about hers.

This is basically what I said...

Casket Chat

"Mom, you took it with you… just like you said you would. And through that decision and the way you chose to communicate it to me, you've taught me a plethora of lessons. I've decided I won't do it like you. I'm leaving it all here. Some day when my three children stand over my casket, they won't have anything to wonder about. There will be no agony of things I've kept from them. They'll laugh for days to come after I'm long gone, about how I sometimes went too far in "letting it all hang out". I can just hear it now! They'll chuckle over the times I spilled all the details, wanting to be so transparent, and they'll wish I'd have toned it down at times. Was it really necessary to tell one of them I conceived them on the beach? Probably not. But that's me. Their lives will be devoid of guess work as far as it depends on me. I've made an intentional decision to never put my children through pain that can be avoided, as far as it depends on me. I'd rather err on the side of sharing too much rather than too little. They will know without a doubt they were accepted for who they are without me trying to change them to what's comfortable for me. I'm not perfect and God knows I've made my share of mistakes, but if there is anything within my power that will take away their pain, it will be their reality without a second thought. I'm doing something else you never did too, and that's get real help. I pursue wholeness and healing at whatever cost for my sake and the sake of my family. There's no cost too great for those I've brought into this world. This will be my legacy Mom, and a huge part of that is because of you. So thanks so much for all you've taught me … and goodbye mom … I love you."

Going Forward

After receiving much help from God, an amazing therapist and the love of my family and friends, my response to the disappointment I have faced in reunion is to build a legacy.

I believe the key when one is disappointed is to get re-appointed.

My reappointment consists of making a choice to be who I'm going to be and not let anyone else decide that for me.

I didn't get a true reunion, and in response I've chosen to build a legacy to leave to my children and everyone my life touches.

Deanna Doss Shrodes is a licensed minister with the Assemblies of God and has served as a pastor for 26 years, along with her pastor-husband, Larry. They have been married for 26 years, have three children and live in the Tampa Bay area where they co-pastor Celebration Church of Tampa. Deanna speaks at churches and conferences internationally and is also an accomplished musician, worship leader, songwriter, and certified coach. An award-winning writer, she is also a contributing author to *Chocolate For a Woman's Courage*, (Simon & Schuster), a contributing author to *Lost Daughters: Writing Adoption from a Place of Empowerment and Peace* (CQT Media and Publishing), and the author of the book *Juggle:Manage Your Time, Change Your Life*.

Deanna blogs at Adoptee Restoration and contributes at Lost Daughters and Adoption Voices Magazine. She leads a search and support group, Adoptee Restoration Tampa Bay and is passionate about providing a safe place for adoptees to heal, as well as expanding the Christian community's understanding of adoption.

Clarity Questions

1. Deanna took several actions in order to help herself find a semblance of closure—the attended therapy, she spoke to her mother's body, and she actively chooses how she is going to live her own life, decidedly free of secrets. What has helped you find closure, acceptance, peace ... however you want to characterize it, regarding the sad, traumatic or tragic things that have happened in your life?

2. Is it a mother's right not to share the father's name? Is it the adult child's right to know the names of his or her parents? Where does this act of secrecy fall—it is a right to privacy (i.e. to not maintain contact), or a right to confidentiality (to keep secrets locked away for all of time)? Were first moms guaranteed confidentiality? Who is benefiting from closed and incomplete records?

Chapter 20

Resurrection

By Mila Konomos

I am two daughters seeking to be one.

I am two people seeking to be one.

I am two of flesh and blood seeking to be one.

I am a thousand pieces longing to be whole.

I am a thousand tears weeping to no longer drown.

I am a thousand questions seeking to be known.

Reunion is like a resurrection. But one that does not happen just once. Rather one that happens over and over, again and again.

For the rest of your life.

And every time you are resurrected, it is nothing like that of Lazarus. No one calls your name to beckon you to arise. And you do not suddenly emerge from the tomb alive and walking and ready to return to life as you know it.

Rather, you are alone. And you do not rise. You crawl. You emerge slowly, painstakingly, excruciatingly. And you can never return to life as you once knew it, because it is no longer there.

Everything has changed.

Rather, again and again, you are resurrected into anguish and sorrow and loss. You are resurrected into separation and confusion and guilt.

Isolation.

Rejection.

Uncertainty.

The pain seems never to cease. The grief resurrects itself time and time again.

When I first began the process of reunion, I was so idealistic. So hopeful. Not that I do not remain hopeful and not that good has not surfaced.

But so much has changed. So much continues to change. It is a storm that endlessly evolves with both horrific beauty and startling peril.

Indeed, the honeymoon phase of reunion ended long ago, and the reality of trying to maintain relationships between people who live on the other side of the world, who do not share a common language, whose cultures diverge, when it feels that so much is at stake, when so much loss and grief have already defined your relationship tangled with the reality that those who raised you, those whom you have called family almost your entire life do not believe in what you are trying to do but rather feel utterly betrayed and would rather you forsake your origins as though they mean nothing—it can feel like a long, slow torture.

A thirst never quenched but only drop by drop. A hunger never fed but only crumb by crumb. An eternal longing never filled but only carved out all the more gapingly and achingly.

It is just as there was always hope waiting at the bottom of Pandora's box, all the horror and terror and pain had to first be set free.

Reunion long-term as a Korean adoptee, at least for me, has become nothing to romanticize or idealize. It is painful and arduous. There are times I want to give up out of exhaustion and disillusionment for trying to overcome the language, cultural, and geographical barriers on top of the already existing emotional barriers to no avail. It's like trying to climb a thousand mountains to get to the other side—and if you were to ever reach the other side, it is no paradise that awaits you.

Even though I have reunited, I still feel so far apart, so distant, so separated.

Reunion has been such a complex experience for me. One that continues to unfold, one that has no end.

Often I do not even know where to begin when people ask me about my reunion.

It is impossible to describe. There are no words.

But here, I will share something I wrote in 2010 after receiving a stirring letter that my Omma (my Korean birth mother) wrote to me upon learning that I was pregnant with my husband's and my first child:

I just received one of the most intense letters from my Omma thus far. She opened up to me for the first time about her memories of her pregnancy and giving birth to me. I learned details about my beginnings, about our beginnings—that is, my Omma's and my beginnings as mother and daughter—that I have never known.

When I traveled to Korea at the end of June last year to reunite with her for the first time in thirty plus years, I had asked her what she remembered from that time. I asked her if she could share with me what it was like for her when she was pregnant with me.

What were her circumstances? What was life like for

her during that time?

When she gave birth to me, was she alone or was someone with her?

Did she ever get to hold me?

She choked up with tears and answered that she could not talk about that time in her life because it was too painful. That was over a year ago.

Perhaps she has chosen to finally open up because she feels more secure, more hopeful that I will be able to better understand her and her circumstances, now that I myself am preparing to give birth.

Perhaps she hopes that my own experience of carrying a child and giving birth will help me to grasp with more compassion and humility, less judgment and condemnation, what and why things unfolded as they did.

But the truth is that I never sought her out to judge her or to condemn her. I never sought her out to accuse or to demand recompense. I sought her out because she and I have always been a part of each other. I sought her out because I wanted to have hope that it is never too late. I sought her out because I wanted to know her and to have a relationship with her, fully aware that pain and sorrow would remain, yet hoping that healing and redemption would overcome.

And now that we are here, now that I have sought her and found her, we both must be patient with one another. Although it is not too late, although we can now know one another and have a relationship with each other, the pain and sorrow that remain make the process of healing and redemption slow and fragile.

Although I begin to feel more assured that things will not again suddenly break apart, the insecurity, the fear of such happening are always there. Hence, there is a timidity and a trepidation with which we both proceed that is not easily overcome. Yet, what matters is that we continue on.

What matters is that she is now allowing herself to open up. And what sorrow and suffering she has known. My heart aches with her as I read her words over and over.

To those who have always known how their lives began, it's easy to take for granted that they can know seemingly mundane details about their beginnings. They can forget how meaningful it is to know that their own mothers held them and nursed them in those first days. They can forget how significant it is to be able to know that they were kissed and caressed by the one who gave them birth. Such details are nothing noteworthy or unique to them, because they have always been assumed.

But to people like me, it is precious, painful treasure. To people like me, it is knowledge that is not so easily assumed but rather questioned and received with angst and hopeful tears.

To discover that I was born by Caesarean is like a golden shard lodged in my throat. To learn for the first time that my Omma and I actually spent the first five days of my life together, as she recovered, is like rubbing jagged jewels in my eyes. Discovering that she nursed me during our brief time together is like a bittersweet elixir sinking into my stomach with the weight of an anvil.

Knowing that we had any time together at all—no matter how short or brief those moments—blankets me as though I am both cold and hot.

And there are deep, secret thoughts that she uttered with her written words that I am not inclined to share.

But to those who would say that the only women who relinquish their children are those who have brought it upon themselves, I would first want to shake you with tears of sorrow and grief choking my rage, pleading with you to open your eyes and mind and heart. But I know that you would not hear me. I know that you would simply dismiss me as crazed and unenlightened. I know that my Omma's story, my Omma's truth would mean nothing to you, because she is only one woman, only one person. And it seems that one is never enough to convince the many.

Instead, life after life must be forfeited until the trail is a grave of losses and sorrows upon sorrows. And even then, the world may continue to pass by, muttering exceptions and rationalizations as it steps over those who have tried time and time again to rise up, but have found no one to believe in them. It is not to say that there are not those who have been so willing to reach out and grasp onto to those who cannot make it alone. But there are still those who remain ignored and despised. My Omma has had to endure such a life.

Of course, she is not perfect. She has not lived a blameless life. But who of us has?

If only the world had been so willing to believe in her as it had been so willing to believe in me. The world saw me as a helpless, innocent child, with no responsibility for the situation thrust upon me. But, ultimately, not one of us is innocent. And ultimately, we all long for mercy rather than judgment.

So, now, every time I feel my son moving in my womb, every time I touch my hand to my abdomen—taut and hard—to feel him pressing against it with a tiny foot or the crown of his head, I think of my Omma. I think of all her sorrow, all her grief, all the pain that she has endured year after year, day after day—a grief and sorrow that both assails and comforts me, because I know, at least I hope I know, that neither my son nor I will ever have to suffer such a fate. And this gives me both a sadness and a pleasure that by knowing the suffering that my Omma and I share, our son will be able to know a depth of wholeness that neither my Omma nor I have ever known.

Clearly, the process of reunion is complex—it is an experience in which joy is laden with ongoing anguish, and hope is burdened with indescribable heartache.

I think the above also exemplifies the constant paradox that adoptees experience, whether reunited or not. However, I believe that being in reunion can intensify the sense of paradox and confusion, which is itself a paradox. One would think that being in reunion would alleviate the confusion and conflict of feeling divided or at odds with oneself. But at least for me, it has served to intensify it whether dealing with identity, family, milestones, or even daily life.

For instance, with landmark moments such as marriage or giving birth to a child—moments that society generally qualifies as joyful and celebratory—for an adoptee, these can elicit deep grief and sorrow, confusion and conflict.

And even more so, when one has reunited, there is a myth, an assumption that reunion will bring complete healing.

To state it clearly—finding one's biological family does *not* fix everything.

It does not make the pain go away. It does not heal the wounds. It does not lift the scars. It does not answer all the questions, and many times, it stirs up even more.

It does not simplify the existing complexities of an adoptee's life. It complicates an identity and experience of family that is already confusing and convoluted.

I know to many I may sound negative and ungrateful. How can you say that? You are so lucky. Do you know how many adoptees long and ache for what you have?

Yes, I know. I know all too well. Finding my biological parents after a seven-year search and coming up on my thirty-fifth birthday, I am very aware of the pain and longing adoptees endure as they search for answers.

I am not saying that I am not fortunate for having the rare chance to connect with my Korean family. I am simply adding to the strange and indescribable experience that as awe-inspiring and wonderful as it may seem to you, it is additionally as equally heart wrenching and terrifying for me.

Again and again, I must learn to live with emotional dissonance, ambiguity, and complexity, seemingly clashing feelings and experiences.

As an adoptee in reunion I live in a constant state of paradox and contradiction.

Every time I must endure resurrection, this is what I am resurrected into.

It is not a new life that I find awaiting me.

It is instead a life of two lives continuously wrestling to be one. Grappling to find wholeness. Struggling to know unity.

Ultimately, I will never give up.

But with every step that I take, I will carry with me always the burden of living life in the paradox of a resurrection that brings both life and death.

Mila C. Konomos is a reunited Korean American transracial adult adoptee. She was born in Seoul, Korea in 1975 and adopted six months later by a White American family. She has been in reunion with her Korean family since 2009. She and her husband have two children. She writes at The Lost Daughters and Yoon's Blur.

Clarity Questions

1. Mila is so incredibly evocative and raw in describing the emotions elicited by her reunion. She says, "It is a storm that endlessly evolves with both horrific beauty and startling peril." In other words, it's complicated. If you are in reunion, how has that complication played out for you?

2. The author relates the joy and pain inherent in her reunion, and yet nowhere does she state that she regrets doing so. What do you make of this reality?

Afterword:

What Will the Adoption Community Do with our Memories?

By Amanda H.L. Transue-Woolston

This afterword is like many afterwords in that it is designed to weave the pieces of the book together while telling the story of how such a work came to be. Unlike other afterwords, this one will not tell you what inspired the editor to embark on an anthology about reunion in the social media age, or describe the process by which she included each one of the incredible authors. Rather, it serves to point out the larger shifting culture of adoption that brings unexpected changes in adoption that this book is evidence of. What do we see in this anthology that I as a 28 year-old (which is relatively young in the adoption community) never thought that I would see? Adoptee voices in the forefront, adoption professionals arguing for openness, original mothers grieving openly, adoptive parents as allies to positive change, and all those from different places in the constellation of adoption working towards holistically acknowledging adoptees—the biological, psychological, social, spiritual, and cultural realities of being adopted. The shift toward these new realities in adoption brought this book to be. This book is part of the shift that will sustain these new realities.

My world shifted when I was 23 and I unknowingly stepped into the larger adoption community also experiencing a shift. I did not know that original mothers grieved their children because I had never met one. I did not know that there are adoption professionals who support openness as a best practice because it was explained to my parents by adoption professionals decades ago that openness should not be an option. I did not know that adoptee voices had value in adoption because almost all of my exposure to adoption in the public eye was led by adoptive parents. I did not know that an integration of my biological heritage from my original family and my social and psychological nurturing experience from my adoptive family was possible because I believed reunion was "off the table" for me. A part of the last generation when closed adoption was considered the only option, at least for private adoption, I was cut off at the roots. Who I was—who my family was—before I was adopted was erased, sealed.

I remember the first time I read a news article of an original mother openly grieving her lost son. I was devastated; I did not want to believe that what I read was real. At one time, I did not know what to make of adoption professionals and adoptive parents arguing for openness and rectification of policy issues. If openness is really best, *why hadn't anyone wanted it for me?* The first time I heard an adoptee openly and boldly talk about their quest for their past—and their difficulties achieving it—I was startled and taken aback. I could not at that time accept their reality because it made me too afraid of my own. I had grown accustomed to the adopted part of myself being boxed and pushed away from my present reality. The adopted part of me lived behind a closed door along with my sealed adoption file and original birth certificate. Facing aspects of adoption that are not neatly boxed and easily pushed aside was like facing a steep cliff I was set to climb. Every chance I gave myself to process this shift in adoption that I was becoming a part of was like adding a foothold to that cliff.

Each author in this book tells a different story; some similar in nature, some very different, but all unique in their own way. Through absorbing their words, we sense their joy and their sorrow, their grief and their solace, and their triumph and steadfastness for the changes they would like to see in adoption. What I will argue is the most important commonality between each author is the fact that these are their memories. Together, these memories make up a larger ocean of memories within the adoption community. Our memories create the history of adoption, and our memories shape the future of adoption. These authors have shared their memories with us; so we ask ourselves, *what now?*

Adoption community members, of all places on the spectrum of feeling positive, negative, or even ambivalent about adoption, spend a great deal of time lending their memories for the good of the community. This is often done to lend support, support what good they see, or to promote change in areas of adoption that need it. Adoptees in-particular sit on adoption question-and-answer panels and have every part of their lives and Selves scrutinized and probed into for the benefit of others. We submit writings to books, anthologies, and other publications. We guest speak at engagements and do workshops in groups. We lend our stories to provide mutual aid in support groups. We put our innermost thoughts about adoption and our adoption experiences on blogs. We allow our legislators insight into our personal histories to compel them to focus on adoption policies. This is typically volunteer work; we don't ask for much more than a few changed laws and lots of listening ears in return.

Our memories are most often exclusively valued for how much they are *of use to someone else*. Furthermore, the societal dichotomization of all adoptions as either "open" or "closed," coupled with the assumption that all adoptions taking place today are "all open now," leads many to discredit those from closed adoption as irrelevant and obsolete. We forget that there are shared experiences across all types of adoptions, there are overarching themes within adoption, and that closed adoption very much still exists. Furthermore, what older community members bring to the table that cannot be offered by anyone else is the experience of living adoption over a length of time. How powerful this is. When we question the relevance of those who have lived adoption, we rob our community of our own rich and powerful resources that could be used to further positive change both in adoption and the world at large.

For adult adoptees, the adoption community is a community chosen for us during a time when we had few choices ourselves. *No one* gets to choose the circumstances they enter into in this life; we all do the best with what we have been given. I know that I am doing the best with my experience with being adopted that I think I can. But the fact remains that it is not about just what we storytellers can give, how we can prove our relevance, and how we can make this community better with our memories. It is time for the adoption community to be inspired to support adoptees and their allies for giving of their time, resources, and memories.

The cultural shift in adoption toward valuing positive change and the voices of adopted people allow me to call for others to honor and recognize our memories, and to be received well by many. The changing tides in adoption not only seek to for policy and practice to be relevant to children and new families in adoption, but to those of us who have been living adoption for a long time. No longer will those of us with undervalued narratives—particularly adoptees and original parents—be required to continue to argue for our own relevancy in adoption. Adoption as an institution must work to maintain relevancy to *our needs*. Our voices will be sought out and honored, such as this anthology portrays. Adoption community members continuously give our memories away to help others and some day, I may need someone to use those memories I gave to help me. Now that you have read their voices, what will you do with their memories?

Amanda H. L. Transue-Woolston is a social worker, author, and speaker. She has an A.A. in psychology, a BSW in social work, and is currently a candidate for a master's in clinical social work. Amanda's work on adoption has appeared in multiple books, magazines, journal articles, radio interviews and has been presented at several conferences. She is a founding board member of the Adoption Policy and Reform Collaborative and also founded Pennsylvania Adoptee Rights and Lost Daughters. Amanda co-facilitates an adoption support group for anyone connected to adoption, and is a quarterly contributor to Gazillion Voices Magazine. Amanda is best known for her internationally recognized, award-winning adoption blog, The Declassified Adoptee.

What's Next?

Thank you so much for reading *Adoption Reunion in the Social Media Age, An Anthology*.

This work is the first of many! Please head over to laura-dennis.com to sign up for the Cool Chick Newsletter. As a member, you'll receive updates on upcoming anthologies, and announcements for free and discounted books. Or, if you want to read more about the editor's own adoption reunion journey, and brief bout with insanity (Hello? Unaddressed post-adoption issues!) click here to read *Adopted Reality, A Memoir* by Laura Dennis.

Biographies

JoAnne Bennett (Contributor)—After being placed for adoption at birth, JoAnne's journey took too many twists and turns to count, and she has spent the last 20 years trying to piece together her missing parts. Nevertheless, JoAnne reflects on her many blessings— raising three wonderful daughters alongside her loving husband of 38 years. Her passions are writing and making a difference in young people's lives. Helping children see that they have voices that truly matter is her heartfelt desire. She believes that loving out loud is a way of positively changing the world. JoAnne's most recent credits include a story in a book titled, *One for the Road,* a publication in *Chicken Soup for the Soul: Teens Talk Middle School,* and on Adoption.Net. She blogs at Stories by JoAnne Bennett.

Addison Cooper, LCSW (Contributor) runs the adoption movie review website, Adoption at the Movies.

He is a foster care adoption supervisor in Southern California. Find him on Facebook, Adoption at the Movies.

Trace A. DeMeyer (Contributor) is the author of *One Small Sacrifice: A Memoir* that details the little-known history of the Indian Adoption Project and the Indian Child Welfare Act; she includes her jaw-dropping journey to find her natural father and tribal relatives. A second book, an anthology *Two Worlds: Lost Children of the Indian Adoption Projects* was published in 2012, co-authored with Patricia Busbee. Her writing has been published in newspapers and journals in the U.S., Canada and Europe. Trace, a graduate of the University of Wisconsin-Superior, has received numerous news and feature writing awards. She lives in Massachusetts and blogs at Trace DeMeyer and Split Feathers.

Laura Dennis (Editor and Contributor) was born and adopted in New Jersey and raised in Maryland. She earned a B.A. and M.F.A. in dance performance and choreography, but gave up aches and pains and bloody feet in 2004 to become a stylish, sales director for a biotech startup. Then with two children under the age of three, in 2010 she and her husband sought to simplify their lifestyle and escaped to his hometown, Belgrade. While the children learned Serbian in their cozy preschool, Laura recovered from sleep deprivation and wrote Adopted Reality, A Memoir, available on Amazon. She blogs at Expat (Adoptee) Mommy.

Deanna Doss Shrodes (Contributor) is a licensed minister with the Assemblies of God and has served as a pastor for 26 years, along with her pastor-husband, Larry. They have been married for 26 years, have three children and live in the Tampa Bay area where they co-pastor Celebration Church of Tampa. Deanna speaks at churches and conferences internationally and is also an accomplished musician, worship leader, songwriter, and certified coach. An award-winning writer, she is also a contributing author to *Chocolate For a Woman's Courage*, (Simon & Schuster), a contributing author to *Lost Daughters: Writing Adoption from a Place of Empowerment and Peace* (CQT Media and Publishing), and the author of the book *Juggle:Manage Your Time, Change Your Life*.

Deanna blogs at Adoptee Restoration and contributes at Lost Daughters and Adoption Voices Magazine. She leads a search and support group, Adoptee Restoration Tampa Bay and is passionate about providing a safe place for adoptees to heal, as well as expanding the Christian community's understanding of adoption.

Daniel Drennan was born in Lebanon and adopted at two months. He grew up in Iran, Australia, and finally the United States, with four years lived in France. In 2004 he returned definitively to Lebanon, and has regained his nationality. Previously he was an assistant professor at the American University of Beirut. He founded the artists' collective Jamma Al-Yad, co-founded the adoptee collective Transracial Eyes, and is a collaborative member of Bada'el/Alternatives (Lebanon), which advocates for the right of children to know their origins. He writes using the pseudonym "Daniel Ibn Zayd."

Becky Drinnen (Contributor) is a baby-scoop-era adoptee who searched for and found her birth parents. Reunion with her birth father and family is a fresh, exciting development in her life. She is also an advocate for adoptee rights. Becky works in corporate America and loves her role as a wife, mom and grandma. In her free time, you'll find her immersed in genealogy research, reading a good history book, or enjoying the great outdoors. Becky blogs about adoption at Puzzles and Possibilities.

Samantha Franklin (Contributor) is a wife, mother, and reunited adoptee. She enjoys spending time with her adoptive and birth family, who all live in the same town in Oklahoma, where she also grew up. Holidays are especially interesting because of this, but so worth it. She is an activist for adoptee access to their original birth certificates and blogs at Neither Here Nor There.

Lynn Grubb (Contributor) is a Baby Scoop Era adoptee who is active in adoptee rights. She is married to Mark—a kind and patient non-adoptee—and lives in a suburb of Dayton, Ohio with their nineteen-year-old son and nine-year-old daughter. Lynn is a paralegal and has volunteered as a Court Appointed Special Advocate (CASA), which ignited her passion for children's rights. Lynn blogs at No Apologies for Being Me and The Lost Daughters.

Rebecca Hawkes (Contributor) is an adult adoptee in reunion and a mother of two daughters (one by birth and one by way of open foster-care adoption). She blogs at Sea Glass and Other Fragments and The Thriving Child. Additionally, she is a contributor at Adoption Voices Magazine and Lost Daughters. She is also a public speaker who has presented at various conferences, together with her adopted daughter's first mother, on the topic of open adoption from foster care. She lives in Western Massachusetts with her husband, her daughters, and a dog named Buddy.

Richard Hill (Contributor) is the author of *Finding Family: My Search for Roots and the Secrets of My DNA*. A decades-long search for his biological family introduced Richard to DNA testing. Motivated to share his success secrets and tips with other adoptees and genealogists, he created his web site, DNA-Testing-

Advisor.com.

As the unifying expert bridging the fields of genetic genealogy and adoption search, he has become the go-to person for adoptees, genealogists, and others seeking to find lost relatives or confirm suspected relationships. His groundbreaking use of genetic genealogy tests was featured on the front page of *The Wall Street Journal*.

Lori Holden (Contributor) writes regularly at LavenderLuz.com about parenting and living mindfully and is a columnist at *The Huffington Post* and at the *Denver Post*'s moms site. She is the author of *The Open-Hearted Way to Open Adoption: Helping Your Child Grow Up Whole*, written with her daughter's birth mom and after listening to adult adoptees and first parents tell of their varied experiences. She lives in Denver with her husband and two tweens and speaks to adoption agencies and their clients about openness in adoption and giving equal access for all citizens to original birth records. She has been known to practice the Both/And mindset when it comes to red wine and dark chocolate.

Mila C. Konomos (Contributor) is a reunited Korean American transracial adult adoptee. She was born in Seoul, Korea in 1975 and adopted six months later by a White American family. She has been in reunion with her Korean family since 2009. She and her husband have two children. Mila blogs at Lost Daughters and Yoon's Blur.

Rhonda Noonan (Contributor) earned an Associate's degree from Northern Oklahoma College, and Bachelors and Masters degrees from Northeastern State University, Tahlequah, Oklahoma. Her career in mental health spans almost thirty years and includes stints as the Director of Clinical Services at five inpatient psychiatric facilities in Oklahoma and Colorado. She has spent much of her career working with adoptees and their families. Find The Fifth and Final Name, Memoir of an American Churchill on Amazon.

Jeanne Nott (Contributor) began entertaining audiences at age five and now, in her sixties, she performs stand-up comedy for seniors. She is an accomplished director and stage performer and was the recipient of an All-State Acting Award at the 2004 Colorado Community Theatre Coalition. Her children's play, *A House is Not a Home*, was presented at the Colorado Performing Arts Festival. Jeanne is also a Colorado Voices writer for The Denver Post. She and her husband, Dr. Paul Crumby, reside in Loveland, Colorado with their dog, "Rolo," who came from Animal Rescue of the Rockies.

Corie Skolnick (Contributor) is the author of *Orfan*, a novel. She is a licensed California Marriage and Family Therapist and has been an adjunct faculty member in the Psychology Departments of both California State University, Northridge (CSUN) and Moorpark College.

The Comparative Literature Program at San Diego State University selected Corie and *Orfan* for the prestigious Hugh C. Hyde Living Writers Series in the Spring of 2012, and Orfan was nominated for the 2012-2013 Freshman Common Reading Selection at Cal State University, Northridge.

Her second novel, *America's Most Eligible* will be published by MVP/MVR in 2014.

Amanda H. L. Transue-Woolston (Afterword) is a social worker, author, and speaker. She has an A.A. in psychology, a BSW in social work, and is currently a candidate for a master's in clinical social work. Amanda's work on adoption has appeared in multiple books, magazines, journal articles, radio interviews and has been presented at several conferences. She is a founding board member of the Adoption Policy and Reform Collaborative and also founded Pennsylvania Adoptee Rights and Lost Daughters. Amanda co-facilitates an adoption support group for anyone connected to adoption, and is a quarterly contributor to Gazillion Voices Magazine. Amanda is best known for her internationally recognized, award-winning adoption blog, The Declassified Adoptee.

Gaye Vale (Contributor) was born and raised in Brisbane, Australia. She is married with three children, two girls aged 30 and sixteen, and a son aged ten, and she recently welcomed her second grand-child to the clan.

Gaye worked in a variety of roles until following her childhood dream to be a teacher. She taught high school for almost a decade, including a year in London. Gaye has been an activist for women's rights for many years and was one of the founders of the women-only political party, the Australian Women's Party in the late 1990s. Gaye now works as a union organizer assisting and supporting school employees, and as her defogging progresses, hopes to gain her voice as an advocate for adoptee rights.

Connect with her via email at gayevale@icloud.com.

Jessie Wagoner Voiers (Contributor) is an adult adoptee in reunion and also mom to six children (one through an open domestic adoption and five bonus children gifted to her upon marriage). She writes about blending families, adoption, parenting, and how to find the humor in the everyday on her blog Then I Laughed. Additionally, Jessie is an advocate for children and families affected by Fetal Alcohol Syndrome